The A to Z of Eating Disorders

Emma Woolf is a writer, broadcaster, former columnist for *The Times* and *Newsweek*, and co-presenter on Channel 4's *Supersize vs Superskinny*. Having studied English at Oxford University, she worked in psychology publishing before going freelance and now writes for a range of newspapers and magazines both in the UK and internationally. She speaks at schools and universities on issues relating to eating disorders and body image, and at literary festivals from Cheltenham to Mumbai. Emma is a regular reviewer on Radio 4's *Saturday Review* and BBC London, and other media appearances include *Newsnight*, *Woman's Hour* and the *Daily Politics* show.

Her first book, *An Apple a Day: A memoir of love and recovery from anorexia*, was translated into many languages. Her other non-fiction titles include *The Ministry of Thin*, *Letting Go*, and *Positively Primal*, and she has also written several novels.

Emma is the great-niece of Virginia Woolf. You can find her on Twitter @EJWoolf.

Overcoming Common Problems Series

Selected titles

A full list of titles is available from Sheldon Press,
36 Causton Street, London SW1P 4ST and on our website at
www.sheldonpress.co.uk

Beating Insomnia: Without really trying
Dr Tim Cantopher

Chronic Fatigue Syndrome: What you need to know about CFS/ME
Dr Megan A. Arroll

Cider Vinegar
Margaret Hills

Coeliac Disease: What you need to know
Alex Gazzola

Coping Successfully with Hiatus Hernia
Dr Tom Smith

Coping with a Mental Health Crisis: Seven steps to healing
Catherine G. Lucas

Coping with Difficult Families
Dr Jane McGregor and Tim McGregor

Coping with Endometriosis
Jill Eckersley and Dr Zara Aziz

Coping with Memory Problems
Dr Sallie Baxendale

Coping with Schizophrenia
Professor Kevin Gournay and Debbie Robson

Coping with the Psychological Effects of Illness
Dr Fran Smith, Dr Carina Eriksen and Professor Robert Bor

Coping with Thyroid Disease
Mark Greener

Depression and Anxiety the Drug-Free Way
Mark Greener

Depressive Illness: The curse of the strong
Dr Tim Cantopher

Dr Dawn's Guide to Brain Health
Dr Dawn Harper

Dr Dawn's Guide to Digestive Health
Dr Dawn Harper

Dr Dawn's Guide to Healthy Eating for Diabetes
Dr Dawn Harper

Dr Dawn's Guide to Healthy Eating for IBS
Dr Dawn Harper

Dr Dawn's Guide to Heart Health
Dr Dawn Harper

Dr Dawn's Guide to Sexual Health
Dr Dawn Harper

Dr Dawn's Guide to Weight and Diabetes
Dr Dawn Harper

Dr Dawn's Guide to Women's Health
Dr Dawn Harper

The Fibromyalgia Healing Diet
Christine Craggs-Hinton

Helping Elderly Relatives
Jill Eckersley

How to Stop Worrying
Dr Frank Tallis

Invisible Illness: Coping with misunderstood conditions
Dr Megan A. Arroll and Professor Christine P. Dancey

Living with Fibromyalgia
Christine Craggs-Hinton

Living with Hearing Loss
Dr Don McFerran, Lucy Handscomb and Dr Cherilee Rutherford

Living with the Challenges of Dementia: A guide for family and friends
Patrick McCurry

Overcoming Emotional Abuse: Survive and heal
Susan Elliot-Wright

Overcoming Low Self-esteem with Mindfulness
Deborah Ward

Overcoming Worry and Anxiety
Dr Jerry Kennard

Post-Traumatic Stress Disorder: Recovery after accident and disaster
Professor Kevin Gournay

The Stroke Survival Guide
Mark Greener

Ten Steps to Positive Living
Dr Windy Dryden

Treating Arthritis: The drug-free way
Margaret Hills and Christine Horner

Understanding High Blood Pressure
Dr Shahid Aziz and Dr Zara Aziz

Understanding Yourself and Others: Practical ideas from the world of coaching
Bob Thomson

When Someone You Love Has Dementia
Susan Elliot-Wright

The Whole Person Recovery Handbook
Emma Drew

Overcoming Common Problems

The A to Z of Eating Disorders

EMMA WOOLF

First published in Great Britain in 2017

Sheldon Press
36 Causton Street
London SW1P 4ST
www.sheldonpress.co.uk

British Library Cataloguing-in-Publication Data
A catalogue record for this book is available from the British Library

ISBN 978-1-84709-461-2
eBook ISBN 978-1-84709-462-9

Typeset by Fakenham Prepress Solutions, Fakenham, Norfolk NR21 8NN
First printed in Great Britain by Ashford Colour Press
Subsequently digitally printed in Great Britain

eBook by Fakenham Prepress Solutions, Fakenham, Norfolk NR21 8NN

Produced on paper from sustainable forests

To Cecil and Jean Woolf

Note to the reader

This is not a medical book and is not intended to replace advice from your doctor. Consult your pharmacist or doctor if you believe you have any of the symptoms described, and if you think you might need medical help.

Introduction

Since I started writing a weekly column in *The Times*, and then my first book *An Apple a Day: A memoir of love and recovery from anorexia* (Summersdale, 2012), I've been contacted by readers around the world who have similar thoughts and feelings – women and men, of all ages and all walks of life, who experience shame about their appetite, guilt with every mouthful, anxiety when eating in public, dislike of their own bodies or just a sense of being out of control around food. An eating disorder can be life-threatening, but everyday disordered eating is also surprisingly common.

Eating disorders are more complex than just diets. The fact remains, however, that the single biggest predictor of developing disordered eating is going on a diet. If the current Western obsession with losing weight – with forever slimming down and toning up, with getting the perfect bikini body or the sculpted six-pack – is to continue, we need to understand the risks, reasons and potential damage that dieting can do. *The A to Z of Eating Disorders* is a practical, comprehensive, no-nonsense, myth-busting guide to all the parts of eating disorders that are hard to understand and hard to explain.

The A to Z is written for those who are struggling with any kind of disordered eating or body-image anxiety, and acknowledges both ends of the spectrum. Whatever your attitude, whatever your weight, modern life has made the simple daily act of eating more complicated than ever before. We are tempted to treat ourselves but told to show restraint, we are urged to indulge while being warned of looming obesity epidemics. Given the contradictions between consumption and deprivation and the nonsense terminology around good and bad foods, clean and dirty eating, virtue or sinfulness, it's no wonder that many of us avoid food, crave it or overdo it. How can we enjoy something that makes us feel so guilty, greedy or fearful?

The A to Z is also a personal project. Although not referring directly to my own illness, clearly my ten years' experience of anorexia and recovery informs everything I write on the subject. I hope my first-hand knowledge will help others to understand how it feels from the inside and reassure those still going through it. I believe that we need to banish many of the inaccurate assumptions about eating disorders. They are not just female problems, they are not just young people's problems – and they are not narcissistic! I am intimately familiar with the shame and secrecy of an eating disorder; they are ugly conditions, they are physically and emotionally self-destructive, and they cause immense pain to others. They are also forms of self-harm. I have not shied away from these more unattractive aspects, because there is a deep need for honesty in this area, as a foundation for recovery.

Science can give us the facts, but it still cannot explain why a starving person will not, cannot, eat. If my experience does anything, I hope it will shine some light on what that feels like from the inside and how to start to break that cycle.

Eating disorders are increasing at an alarming rate. The statistics speak for themselves: a 34 per cent increase in admissions for inpatient care since 2006; an annual increase of 12 per cent in children being treated in hospital for eating disorders; exponential increases among boys and young men, with up to 25 per cent of those affected now thought to be male; girls as young as six years old saying they feel 'fat' or dislike their bodies, and girls under ten starting on the lifelong cycle of dieting.

Nor is it only the young who are affected: a 2017 study from University College London made headlines with its findings that a 'significant' number of women in their forties and fifties had an active eating disorder, and 15 per cent of them had experienced an eating disorder at some point in their lifetime. National Health

Service (NHS) research estimates that up to 6.4 per cent of UK adults display signs of an eating disorder. With the cost of illness and treatment potentially as high as £15 billion a year, eating disorders are now acknowledged to be a major concern within the medical, psychiatric and public health community.

Along with anorexia nervosa and bulimia nervosa, less well-known conditions are proliferating, including orthorexia, binge-eating disorder (BED) and other ED-NOS (eating disorders not otherwise specified). In the mainstream media, the debate over clean eating and extreme restrictive dieting continues – as it does at the other end of the spectrum in relation to the so-called 'epidemic' of obesity and its medical and financial implications.

There is no doubt that mental illness has risen up the agenda in recent years, with more awareness on the part of medical professionals, more attention from politicians and public health officials and more coverage in the media. For too long, people with mental illnesses have struggled alone, experiencing shame, guilt and confusion about their private problems. With this increased exposure and discussion, however, comes a need for accurate information and authentic real-life testimony.

Mental illnesses, especially eating disorders, cannot necessarily be diagnosed from a medical encyclopaedia or treated with a simple pill. Psychiatric conditions such as anorexia, bulimia and BED are still widely misunderstood. Research is at a relatively early stage and the complex interplay between the physical and the mental aspects remain a mystery to many (including those affected). The roots of any eating disorder are complex and specific to each case, and what works for one person in recovery may not work for another. Anorexia, bulimia and other behavioural disorders are a minefield from the inside and a mystery from the outside. This A to Z aims to bridge the gap between psychology and everyday life, demystifying the key issues and terminology and giving everyone the confidence to deal with these complex conditions.

One thing is clear: eating disorders are about much more than just food or body weight. This A to Z explores the subject from a wide range of angles – physiological and psychological, body and mind, head and heart, emotional, social, medical and nutritional. Whatever the disorder, the impact on an individual's life is considerable. It affects not only physical health but also education or career, friendships, professional interactions and intimate relationships. Food is ever-present in our society, and eating with others is an everyday social bonding experience. To find oneself trapped in the cycle of disordered eating can be intensely isolating. Eating disorders are a heavy burden to carry.

I have balanced the coverage between anorexia nervosa, bulimia nervosa, BED and other ED-NOS. Of course these conditions do not fit under neat labels and people commonly present with a range of different behaviours, sometimes restricting and at other times bingeing and purging. I've explored the issues around body image – from simple confidence and self-esteem, to the more serious body dysmorphic disorder (BDD). I've also looked at less common conditions, such as childhood eating disorders and night-eating syndrome. In addition, I have touched on the recent findings of neurobiological research into eating disorders, which is promising but still at an early stage.

Eating disorders affect not only the person but also the entire family. This A to Z is written with an awareness of parents and siblings, friends and partners. Few conditions are as disruptive to family life as eating disorders: as well as creating tension at mealtimes, there are the deceit, secrecy and subterfuge that surround a disordered relationship with food. Many parents of young people with eating disorders blame themselves for the illness and wonder what they did wrong. While the stress on families is considerable, they are also an invaluable source of support and love during the recovery process.

One of the most important findings to come out of research in this area is that eating disorders are emphatically not confined to teenage girls. They can affect anyone, of any age, gender, sex or social class. From the young man fighting anorexia to the middle-aged mother struggling with BED to the elderly man hiding bulimia, disordered eating can be a way of coping with loneliness, depression or even boredom. It may be a reaction to serious trauma or abuse or it may simply develop from the cycle of deprivation and excess of constant dieting. There are no rules respecting who gets ill and, sadly, as yet, no cure.

Greater awareness around eating disorders has coincided with the explosion of social media and all that goes along with it, notably the sheer visibility of bodies – especially women's bodies – everywhere every day. We are bombarded with thousands of images on celebrity gossip sites, of digitally retouched bodies in advertising and endless selfies on Instagram, Twitter and Facebook. Although the online world has given many lonely people a voice, enabling them to write about their personal experiences and struggles through blogs and internet forums, it has also fuelled the compare-and-despair cycle that makes many young people feel inadequate, scrolling through other people's apparently perfect lives. The internet has also enabled the proliferation of dangerous 'pro-ana' and 'pro-mia' websites which glamorize and even promote conditions such as anorexia and bulimia nervosa.

As incidence and awareness have grown, so has the need for accurate information. Eating disorders may be on the public agenda, but they remain widely misunderstood. Let's be honest, eating disorders are almost impossible to understand from the outside. In severe anorexia, for example, it seems incomprehensible that these people could truly believe they are overweight or not accept how desperately they need to eat. Because the consequences are often shockingly visible – emaciation or obesity – eating disorders are seen as *physical* illnesses. It is assumed that these individuals are obsessed with being thin and attaining the perfect body or they're inordinately greedy and have no self-control. In most cases, however, restricting, bingeing and purging and compulsive overeating have their roots in difficult emotions or other painful problems. In this A to Z, I have emphasized the psychological – as much as the physical – aspects of eating disorders.

It must also be noted that eating disorders are not always visible. Conditions such as bulimia nervosa do not necessarily lead to marked weight gain or loss; many people remain a normal weight despite disrupted and dangerous purging behaviours. Sadly, this means that the problems remain hidden and untreated.

This element of secrecy is common to almost all disordered eating. Although every individual and every illness is different, they share this overwhelming sense of shame, guilt and secrecy. Whether they are anorexic, bulimic or binge-eating, people feel embarrassed about their struggles and ashamed to ask for help. They pretend they're OK because it seems silly to admit they can't cope. Also, whether undereating or overeating, there is a sense of being out of control around food, of trying to regain control or impose order on a situation that feels unmanageable (in anorexia, say) or of giving up and burying one's emotions in food (as in BED).

As well as providing factual information and the latest research, I hope the A to Z will reassure anyone with *any* eating disorder that it is not a life sentence. Although it must be acknowledged that these are life-threatening conditions, they can be overcome. Whether you're at your lowest point of the illness or well on your way to full recovery, I want you to believe that it can be beaten. From overweight to underweight, overeating to undereating, bingeing, purging, constantly dieting or just privately hating your body, you are not alone. The experience of disordered eating is bewildering and lonely, but there is nothing to be ashamed of, and there is great strength in asking for help.

A word on terminology. In the interests of brevity, I have mostly used the term 'individual', 'person' or 'people' to describe the person with the eating disorder. This seems preferable to the terms 'anorexic', 'bulimic' or 'binge-eater' – although I sometimes use them – but I'm aware how reductive these labels can feel. You are a person, not an eating disorder, a mental illness or a collection of symptoms. Please be assured, in every case I simply mean 'the individual with the eating disorder' and do not wish to define or stigmatize anyone.

I hope that this A to Z will carry you from illness to recovery with determination and optimism, and I wish you well on your journey back to health.

a

ADDICTION

The term 'addiction' usually refers to some kind of illegal or damaging behaviour. Food is a completely legal substance and eating is a normal social activity. Food, however, is also a deeply personal issue and disordered eating encompasses a wide range of complicated and individual behaviours. Just like oxygen, food is a fundamental physiological requirement, but we have made eating far more complicated than breathing. We all need food in order to stay alive, but what, when and how much we eat can easily get out of control.

For someone with an eating disorder, food is often both a best friend and a worst enemy. Eating can be a reward and a punishment, consoling and confusing, comforting and guilt-inducing, all at the same time. Starving, purging or bingeing to the point of sickness are painful and pointless behaviours, yet they are self-inflicted (at least at the start). The question is: why would anyone choose such behaviour and how does it become addictive?

Conditions such as anorexia nervosa, bulimia nervosa and BED are highly complex mental illnesses and stubbornly resistant to treatment. Unlike a drug or alcohol addiction, beating an eating disorder is not a simple case of avoiding the substance altogether: you have to learn to eat in order to live.

Eating disorders also bring other problems with them. Alcohol and drug abuse, overspending and even shoplifting (see **KLEPTOMANIA**) are common co-addictions, or dual disorders, in those with disordered eating. It appears that many of the emotional factors fuelling these problematic behavioural patterns are similar.

These factors may include guilt, hunger, boredom or a need to find an escape route from difficult feelings. Drugs or alcohol may be used initially to numb depression or anxiety or help with sleeping problems.

Exercise addiction is also extremely common in those with eating disorders. In recent years, exercise has become more intense than ever before and it has become fashionable to work out really hard, for women as well as for men. A swim or aerobics session no longer cuts it: instead gyms offer a wide choice of 'bootcamp' workouts, circuit training and spin classes. Kick-boxing and military-style fitness classes are full of very toned, fit, thin individuals burning hundreds of calories early in the morning or late at night, often on little fuel. Participation in marathons, triathlons and Iron Man competitions has soared as 'normal' non-athletes push themselves further and further.

It is difficult for outsiders – friends, family, even medical professionals – to accept that an eating disorder and compulsive exercise can be such powerful addictions, but there is growing evidence to suggest that they really are. While exercising regularly and eating healthily are beneficial for most people, in vulnerable individuals they can easily become dangerous, compulsive and sometimes life-threatening addictions.

ALCOHOL

As we have seen, eating disorders often go hand in hand with other forms of addiction and substance abuse, including alcohol.

Individuals with restrictive eating habits such as anorexia are wary of calories in all forms and many of them avoid drinking alcohol for the 'empty calories' it contains. Still, it's estimated that around 15 to 20 per cent of those with anorexia drink excessive amounts of alcohol. In other eating disorders, however, such as bulimia and BED, alcohol abuse is more common, affecting between 30 and 50 per cent of those with binge–purge behaviours. Just as with food, these individuals commonly drink large quantities of alcohol in sporadic binge sessions.

Occasional overindulgence is part of Western culture – getting tipsy at large social events is considered normal, for example – but repeated binge-drinking is far more serious. Many who have BED and bulimia are also affected by substance abuse disorders. A combination of chemical, psychological and sociocultural factors makes them even more vulnerable to addiction. Just as high levels of sugar and fat in binge-eating cause an initial dopamine surge in the brain, so the first few alcoholic drinks create a feeling of euphoria and confidence. People may find themselves bingeing more and more frequently on food and alcohol because they crave that intense rush of chemicals. If they have low dopamine levels – common in those with slight to moderate depression – the dopamine rush seems to lift their depressed mood.

In situations of stress or anxiety, common in everyday life, individuals predisposed to BED or alcoholism may find themselves turning to alcohol or other drugs as a coping mechanism. As with many aspects of an eating disorder, the initial behaviour sets up a cycle of deprivation, craving, excess and guilt. Low self-esteem and low impulse control contribute to problems with alcohol and other substance abuse.

Alcohol abuse is always a cause for concern, but it's particularly dangerous in those who are malnourished, underweight, vomiting frequently or drinking on an empty stomach. It can cause alcohol poisoning, memory loss, blackouts, injuries, brain damage and even death. (See also **DRUNKOREXIA**.)

ALEXYTHYMIA

This describes the generalized difficulties of putting feelings into words seen in some individuals with anorexia. Although often highly intelligent and otherwise articulate, they may struggle to express their emotions and distinguish between facts and feelings. This may be due to specific cognitive deficits associated with anorexia (see **COGNITIVE IMPAIRMENT**) or it may be due to the many conflicting emotions they experience around food, eating and their own bodies.

ALL-OR-NOTHING MINDSET

See **COGNITIVE IMPAIRMENT**.

ALTERNATIVE AND COMPLEMENTARY THERAPIES

Many people find alternative or complementary therapies effective for dealing with a range of physical and emotional issues. From acupuncture, aromatherapy, homeopathy and naturopathy to massage, reflexology, meditation and mindfulness, complementary therapies are based on a belief in the body's ability to heal itself. In general, they adopt an holistic approach to the workings of the body, taking into account the mind–body balance. They are thought to be less invasive than conventional medicine and cause fewer unpleasant side effects.

In theory, eating disorders should respond well to complementary therapies. Anorexia, bulimia and other forms of disordered eating have a significant psychological component, which should make them ideally suited to this more holistic, person-centred approach. Clinical research into complementary therapies in relation to eating disorders is limited, however, and therefore evidence-based data are lacking. As alternative or complementary therapies fall outside mainstream health care, they are generally offered by private practitioners.

Evidence suggests that individuals with severely disordered eating respond best to psychotherapy and other talking therapies, as well as nutritional counselling. Anecdotally, however, many people find complementary, holistic mind–body treatments effective for coping with depression and anxiety, which lie at the root of many eating disorders, or find them beneficial during times of emotional stress and anxiety. Complementary practitioners tailor their treatments to the individual, listening to address specific physical or psychological concerns, and can offer a genuine boost to individuals struggling with eating disorders, but these approaches are not sufficient as stand-alone treatments. They contribute to general health, both mental and physical, and can help with hormonal or nutritional imbalances. They can promote a sense of mental well-being, relaxation and calm. In conjunction with conventional medicines and talking therapies, therefore, complementary therapies can help during the recovery process.

Some herbal treatments can interact with other medications so you should always consult your doctor or counsellor before embarking on complementary or alternative therapies.

AMENORRHOEA

This is a condition in which periods are absent. There are many reasons why periods may be missed, but in the context of eating disorders, we will focus on weight-related causes.

If you are not pregnant, breastfeeding or approaching the menopause, you should be menstruating on a regular 'monthly' cycle (cycles shorter or longer than this are normal, however). Missing periods for several months in a row, and certainly for more than six months, is a cause for concern, though, and should be discussed with your GP.

Essential hormones that control the female menstrual cycle are very sensitively balanced and easily upset when body fat, calories, energy or activity levels become imbalanced. Body fat is essential for the female reproductive system to function, and women need adequate stores of body fat in case of pregnancy. Amenorrhoea is common in anorexia, as well as in those who are underweight or have lost a large amount of weight rapidly. This absence of periods may be the first sign that something is wrong.

When calories are being severely restricted, the body's warning systems go off. The body goes into famine mode, concentrating all its precious resources on keeping it alive. Calories are channelled towards the vital organs and non-essential functions, such as the reproductive system, shut down. To put it simply, with barely enough food for one person, let alone two, the anorexic body cannot risk getting pregnant.

It is generally agreed that body fat needs to be around 17 per cent for menstruation – this explains why female athletes who have a higher than normal muscle-to-fat ratio may miss periods. Even though their calorie intake is high, their energy expenditure is also high and their body fat is low. (See also **ATHLETIC TRIAD** and **EXERCISE**.) Some put the figure for body fat lower: the American College of Sports Medicine, for example, gives a range of 8 to 12 per cent essential body fat to maintain menstruation. While low body fat contributes to menstrual dysfunction and amenorrhoea, it's clear that other factors, such as low calorie intake, inadequate nutrition and excessive exercise, are also highly significant.

In overweight women, there is more than enough body fat, but this can also cause menstrual disturbances, as increased amounts of body fat are related to low levels of sex hormone-binding globulin – a protein that governs the activities of the sex hormones oestrogen and testosterone. Although most oestrogen is produced by the ovaries, some is made in body fat and other sites, and body fat also acts as an oestrogen store. Too much fat therefore causes hormonal imbalance, which disrupts normal egg development and ovulation. Polycystic ovary syndrome is also a common cause of amenorrhoea and can be alleviated by weight loss.

The good news is that, for both overweight and underweight individuals, amenorrhoea is largely reversible. Losing excess weight, or regaining healthy weight, is highly effective at restoring healthy hormone balance. When weight and body fat are at healthy levels – not too high and not too low – hormone levels return to normal, stimulating ovulation and regular periods (see also **FERTILITY AND INFERTILITY**). However, young girls who have primary amenorrhoea, whose periods never start, may permanently damage their reproductive system and never menstruate as adults.

ANAEMIA

Anaemia occurs when the body's red blood cell count is lower than normal. The body needs iron to produce red blood cells, which help store and transport oxygen around the body. When red blood cell levels are low, the body's organs and tissues do not receive as much oxygen as they need. Symptoms of anaemia include fatigue or lethargy, shortness of breath, dizziness or muscle weakness, skin pallor, repeated infections or illness, depression, confusion and poor memory. (See also **IRON**.)

The most common form of anaemia – iron deficiency anaemia (caused by insufficient or poor absorption of iron) – is often seen in eating disorders. In anorexic individuals, iron deficiency may be caused by the general nutritional deficiencies of a restrictive diet. Additionally, these individuals are often vegetarian or vegan, thus avoiding animal products, which are a reliable source of iron. In bulimia, bingeing and purging behaviours lead to iron deficiencies due to repeated vomiting and the disrupted digestion and absorption of food.

Iron deficiency anaemia is straightforward to diagnose and treat and, in most cases, simple iron supplementation is sufficient. (See also **VITAMIN B GROUP**.) In anaemia linked to eating disorders, symptoms will improve as nutritional balance is restored in line with overall physical recovery. Food sources of iron include dark green leafy vegetables, brown rice, pulses, beans, nuts, seeds, iron-fortified cereals and bread, meat, fish, tofu, eggs and dried fruits, such as dried apricots or prunes.

ANOREXIA NERVOSA

The literal meaning of the original Greek is 'nervous loss of appetite'. Anorexia nervosa is characterized by distorted body image, excessive dieting, severe restriction of calories, avoidance of food, extreme or rapid weight loss and a pathological fear of gaining weight. Individuals with anorexia may persist in the belief that they are fat even when they have become dangerously thin. Although anorexia is often diagnosed on the basis of this very low body weight, it should be remembered that it is a psychiatric disorder: the characteristic preoccupation with thinness and restriction of food can exist even in those who are not – or not yet – clinically underweight.

Along with avoidance of energy intake, people with anorexia are also dominated by an intense need to expend energy. They are overcome with guilt about anything that breaks their self-imposed rules.

They find it very hard to respond to their body's physical needs, even simple needs such as warmth, rest and food. As anorexia develops, previously enjoyable activities, such as sport, become compulsive and self-destructive; the person is driven to increase the duration and intensity of exercise to damaging levels. Rigid discipline and self-control, especially around food and exercise, come to dominate the person's life.

The peak average age of onset of anorexia is between 15 and 19 years old. Anorexia has a strong preponderance among female members of the population, with an overall sex ratio of around 10:1 female:male, although in adolescence this ratio varies greatly and there is a growing incidence among young men (see **MALES**). Anorexia is a varied, complex and multifactorial disorder, with no single cause. Every person will present with his or her own specific life circumstances, but will also share many traits in common with others with anorexia. Biological, psychological, sociocultural and neurological research in recent years has contributed greatly to the understanding and diagnosis of anorexia nervosa. It is also increasingly understood that eating disorders have different aspects. That is, there are *predisposing* factors that may make an individual vulnerable; *precipitating* factors that may trigger or encourage disordered eating; and *perpetuating* factors that help to maintain the disorder once it has started.

As research has developed, the diagnosis of anorexia has developed too. Previous editions of the American Psychiatric Association's *Diagnostic and Statistical Manual of Mental Disorders* (see **DSM**) outlined strict medical criteria for anorexia, such as having amenorrhoea (absence of periods) for at least three months or losing a certain percentage of body weight. In the latest edition of the DSM (5th edition, 2013), however, the criteria for anorexia nervosa were changed and amenorrhoea is no longer a requirement. The individual's behaviour and emotional state are considered to be more relevant. This change reflects an important shift in understanding among those in the medical community: anorexia is not defined only by what individuals weigh but also how they feel about their own bodies, eating patterns and behaviour.

In most cases of anorexia, the focus is not solely on food, weight and shape. Other preoccupations include control and self-discipline, perfectionism, self-esteem, identity, sexuality, family, cognitive rigidity and many other issues not directly related to food.

ANOSOGNOSIA

This is a feature often seen in anorexia, where individuals display a lack of awareness of their illness or deny that they are ill. This is common when anorexic people are admitted to hospital but still maintain they do not have a problem with eating. They may not understand the true extent of their illness or they may explain their severely restrictive diet as just being healthy eating. Anosognosia is not the same as hiding a problem, such as in bulimia, where a person understands that his or her behaviour is problematic but is keeping it secret.

Some (but not all) anorexic individuals have a distorted view of what they see in the mirror. They may see themselves as normal weight or even overweight, although outsiders can clearly see they are dangerously underweight.

Anosognosia in eating disorders is confusing as individuals often fluctuate between having insight into the situation and other times when they are in denial. This type of shifting insight presents a challenge for clinicians working with people in therapy. It is also difficult for families, friends and partners of individuals who are severely unwell, as it may feel like progress is not being made.

ANTIDEPRESSANTS AND DEPRESSION

Everyone feels sad, hopeless or anxious at times. This is a normal part of life's ups and downs for all of us, especially when we're faced with work, exam or relationship stresses, or unforeseen events, such as bereavement or serious illness. Depression, however, sometimes has no specific cause and does not pass with time. Antidepressant medication is prescribed when an individual is struggling with moderate or severe depression that doesn't lift naturally. As well as extremely low mood, individuals may experience difficulty sleeping, lethargy, poor appetite and decreased libido, as well as a general sense of despair or even suicidal thoughts. Medication, often in conjunction with support or counselling, can be very effective in these cases. Antidepressants may have to be taken for many months and treatment should not be stopped too soon, as symptoms are likely to reappear.

Depression is thought to be caused by a reduction of certain chemicals in the brain called neurotransmitters, which affect mood by stimulating brain cells. Antidepressants increase the level of these excitatory neurotransmitters, usually by blocking their reabsorption. Three main classes of drugs are used to treat depression: tricyclic antidepressants, selective serotonin reuptake inhibitors (SSRIs) and monoamine oxidase inhibitors (MAOIs).

Depression is very common in individuals with eating disorders. There are many reasons for this (explored in detail throughout this book): depression may be a cause or a consequence. The depressed mood may be something the individual has struggled with for a long time; it may in the end be hard to disentangle it from the eating disorder itself. Conditions such as anorexia, bulimia or binge-eating are also inherently depressing: they create daily anxiety and isolate you from friends and family. Eating disorders make normal situations – such as shopping or eating out – feel stressful or threatening.

Individuals with eating disorders often have low self-esteem and may feel they do not 'deserve' to be OK. They may resist the medication that is offered to help alleviate their depression. They may also fear the side effects, such as weight gain. It's essential to understand that depression makes recovery even harder, and essential to accept that antidepressants are an important part of beating the eating disorder. Depression is not something to be ashamed of – in fact it's surprisingly common. Taking antidepressants does not make you a failure. Boosting those neurotransmitters in your brain makes a real difference to the feelings of hopelessness and despair. By lifting the depressed mood, you can start to see and think more clearly and take positive steps towards normalizing your eating.

ANXIETY

Anxiety is a natural and necessary part of everyday life, with worries or nerves affecting most people at some point. Experiencing anxiety around exams, job interviews or first dates is perfectly normal. 'Normal' levels of anxiety sometimes get out of control, however, affecting the individual both physically and mentally and interfering with daily life. Anxiety is the body's evolutionary response to threatening situations: when it senses a potential threat, the brain triggers the adrenal glands to release adrenaline into the bloodstream. The adrenaline rushes to the heart, lungs and muscles, increasing energy and oxygen levels in preparation for a fight or flight. Tension, a racing heartbeat and sweating are signs that your body is preparing to respond to a perceived threat.

Anxiety is considered abnormal when it is out of proportion to the stressful situation, the anxiety persists after the stressful situation is over or it occurs for no apparent reason. When anxiety feels unmanageable and interferes with daily life, this is considered an anxiety disorder. People with an anxiety disorder may struggle to control their thoughts and feel an overwhelming sense of dread or panic, often alongside distressing physical symptoms. They experience anxiety most days and find it hard to recall a time when they felt relaxed.

The World Health Organization estimates that 1 in 3 people will experience depression or an anxiety disorder at some point in their lives. Research from the University of Cambridge (2016) estimates that more than 60 million people are affected by anxiety disorders every year in the European Union. Anxiety is the primary symptom in a range of related conditions, including obsessive compulsive disorder (OCD), generalized anxiety disorder, post-traumatic stress disorder, social anxiety disorder, phobias and panic disorder.

Physical manifestations of anxiety include sweating, shaking or tremors, shortness of breath, flushing or burning skin, dry mouth, hyperventilating, palpitations or elevated heart rate, chest tightness or stomach pain, nausea, headache and dizziness. Triggers, causes and symptoms of anxiety are wide-ranging and unique to each individual. What may trigger a panic attack in one person may not affect another.

Anxiety disorders have many causes, from brain chemistry to childhood experiences, genetics, habits, diet, medication, major or minor life events and sleep patterns. An individual's temperament plays a role: some of us are naturally more anxious than others. Often the precise trigger for the anxiety is not clear or is something very minor, and the level of anxiety felt can be out of proportion to the trigger itself. Social media use may exacerbate feelings of anxiety or panic: in surveys, 45 per cent of young people say that social media leaves them feeling 'worried and uncomfortable'.

In the context of eating disorders, people may experience intense anxiety around food and social eating situations: it could be a restaurant, a supermarket or a hotel buffet, a work dinner or a picnic with friends. Whether food is experienced as a threat, as in anorexia, or as a trigger, as in binge-eating, many of these everyday eating situations induce extreme anxiety. This makes sense: the more you avoid a situation or feel out of control, the more anxiety builds up around it. Unfortunately, avoiding situations only leads to greater fear and social exclusion (see **LONELINESS**).

COGNITIVE BEHAVIOURAL THERAPY (CBT) is usually the first line of treatment for anxiety disorders and can be very effective. On your own, simple mindfulness techniques and deep breathing can prove very helpful in reducing levels of anxiety and arousal (see also **YOGA**).

It must also be noted that disordered eating exacerbates anxiety, in a nutritional sense. The brain does not function well without good fuel: in particular, the neurotransmitter serotonin, which regulates mood and checking behaviours, is affected. Insufficient intake of carbohydrates can lead to serotonin depletion, which contributes to feelings of anxiety. Eating good-quality carbohydrates is therefore essential for those with anxiety disorders (see also **OBSESSIVE COMPULSIVE DISORDER** and **SEROTONIN**). Noradrenaline is another essential neurotransmitter that is strongly implicated in anxiety disorders (see **NORADRENALINE**).

APPETITE

The Greek term *anorexia nervosa* misleadingly suggests a lack or loss of appetite. Although individuals with anorexia do not in fact start out by losing their appetite, over time the repeated disordered behaviours can confuse the body's natural appetite cues and hunger signals. Similarly, individuals with bulimia or BED may struggle to identify with their appetite or hear when their body is hungry as they are eating large quantities of food in response to emotional, not physical, needs. In all forms of disordered eating, the body's natural appetite is repeatedly confused, ignored or overridden. Getting back in touch with your appetite is crucial to recovery from any eating disorder. (See also **HUNGER**.)

ATHLETES

See **EXERCISE**.

ATHLETIC TRIAD

The female athletic triad refers to the combination of three conditions seen in female athletes: disordered eating, amenorrhoea and osteoporosis. The triad reflects the dangerous consequences of intense physical training, low calorie intake and low body fat, and can result in cessation of menstrual periods, low bone density, infertility and other health problems. Although these are often seen together, an athlete may have only one of these conditions.

BALANCE

Striking a balance is harder than it sounds. Life can sometimes feel like a constant balancing act between work and play, career and family, duty and pleasure, food and exercise, discipline and indulgence. As we grow up, most of us are trying to maintain a happy medium between what we *want* to do and what we *ought* to do: what we need for ourselves and what others need from us, as well as what would be best for our own health and our future prospects. You may look around you and think that everyone else is finding it easy – but balance is hard for all of us.

Modern life, and especially *online* modern life, promises us instant gratification just one click away. It offers countless flavours, brands, destinations, styles and filters, and countless possible versions of ourselves. Navigating our way through this minefield can be bewildering, and often it all gets too much.

Imbalance is at the heart of most disordered eating behaviours, in many different forms. The imbalance may be the all-or-nothing mindset, where a strict diet or exercise regime is taken to dangerous extremes; it may be binge-eating or bingeing and purging. The person wonders why everyone else is apparently able to eat normally, not too little and not too much, while they swing from one extreme to the other. The emotional toll of eating disorders is driven by this lack of balance, where the dominant emotion is guilt at one's own extreme behaviour, shame at being selfish or narcissistic, or worry over creating so much anxiety for family and friends. The individual is all too aware of his or her imbalanced emotional, behavioural and eating patterns, yet feels powerless to change.

Balance sounds very simple, and is not simple at all. *Striving* towards balance, however, is achievable. In the cycle of disordered eating, individuals often finds themselves pulled between extremes. Understanding that a little indulgence is possible can be a revelation for someone with long-term disordered eating. Harmony, indulgence, pleasure and treats are part of a balanced life, even for those who have lost their way.

It's not only individuals with eating disorders who have a sense of imbalance. The endless possibilities and varieties can make even 'normal' individuals feel that there are simply too many potential alternatives, in restaurants, in supermarkets, at college or in the workplace, and of course online. This is known as the paradox of choice: a kind of paralysis in our *more more more* world. When everything is available, it can be hard to choose. Finding an inner equilibrium is tricky when the world appears to offer so much.

Individuals with eating disorders tend to experience this sensation of being overwhelmed, unable to choose from all the possibilities, frozen in the headlights. In anorexia, the perfectionist tendency makes them terrified of making the wrong choice, eating the wrong thing – hence they reject it all. Bulimics often experience a similar sense of overload, and they respond by overdoing it, and then trying to get rid of it all, literally to purge themselves. Disordered eating takes many forms, but the imbalance is the same.

You may remember an old saying, 'a little of what you fancy does you good'. It's simple and true. We live in an obsessively self-controlled society: in food, in exercise, in how we should look and even how we should feel. We're constantly reminded to avoid wheat, dairy or gluten, to wear this, to drink that, to be calmer, more serene, more mindful. We should be a slave to our Fitbit or personal trainer and have perfectly toned abs. We are surrounded by rules and standards and judgement and guilt. We tell ourselves we are not 'allowed' certain things and use food as punishment or reward. It's not surprising that, with or without an eating disorder, anxiety is on the increase.

There are no easy answers, but there are ways to make the balancing act a little easier. Most importantly, stop seeing things as 'good' and 'bad'; instead aim for somewhere in the middle. This is hard in a society that demonizes everyday substances such as dairy or grains and evangelizes 'clean eating'. The 80/20 rule is an excellent guideline for being healthy most of the time, but also allowing yourself treats. This goes for eating but also for exercise regimes: regular activity is important, but the body also needs days off to recover.

Whatever you follow, don't follow it slavishly! Individuals with eating disorders, especially anorexia, have *too many rules* already. The essence of balance is cutting yourself some slack. No meal, no workout, no body will ever be 'perfect'; good enough, healthy enough, happy enough is fine. Aim for moderation and see where it takes you.

BIGOREXIA

This is a form of **BODY DYSMORPHIC DISORDER (BDD)** in individuals, usually men, who spend a lot of time weight training in gyms and seems to be becoming increasingly common. Bigorexia is also referred to as 'muscle dysmorphia' or 'reverse anorexia'. As well as becoming obsessed with bodybuilding, individuals experience distorted perceptions of their body shape and size and may risk their health with steroid abuse. They lift weights compulsively in order to bulk up, but continue to see themselves as weak and skinny, no matter how muscular they become. This kind of excessive training regime exerts a physical strain on the body, especially dangerous in conjunction with steroids, and often causes mental distress, such as depression, anxiety and even suicide.

Research shows that up to 1 in 10 men in gyms could have bigorexia, although the condition is often hidden due to shame. It's still hard for men to admit to struggling with mental health issues, especially those connected with what might be seen stereotypically as 'feminine' problems around body image.

Just as society and the media create pressures on women to be thin and have the perfect body, so they also create pressures on men to display the chiselled torso and perfect six-pack. Typically, a man with bigorexia will work out compulsively, sometimes visiting the gym twice a day, to the exclusion of his social life, study or career, family and relationships. He may become overly concerned with his appearance and have very low self-esteem.

Signs of muscle dysmorphia or bigorexia may include: constantly visiting the gym or lifting weights at home, and becoming panicky or angry if they cannot do this; exercising despite injury or illness; extreme preoccupation with appearance, especially muscle definition in the torso and upper body; consuming large quantities of bodybuilding supplements and protein shakes; and depression, anxiety, irritability or mania. A significant proportion of men will take anabolic steroids to maximize their muscle growth. Side effects of steroid abuse include mood swings, aggression, hair loss, impotence, testicle shrinkage and heart and liver damage.

As with other mental illnesses (see **MYTHS AND MISUNDER-STANDINGS**), bigorexia is widely misunderstood. It is seen as narcissistic posing, whereas in fact it is a serious form of body-image distortion. It often masks insecurities in other areas of an individual's life. As with anorexia, bigorexia involves a mismatch between the person's internal self-perception (as effeminate or weedy) and the external reality of a very muscular man.

This kind of body dysmorphia may develop as a result of childhood abuse, trauma or bullying at school, or it may be a response to the unrealistic expectations created by the modern media. Male models display the 'perfect body' and create pressures on men, similar to those on women, to achieve the same physique. While it used to be characterized as a particular issue for gay men, who were thought to be closer to women in their concern over appearance, it is now clear that body dysmorphia can affect all men, gay or straight, young or old.

Intriguingly, male body dysmorphia is almost the exact opposite of female anorexia: where women shrink themselves into nothingness, men are trying to increase their physical presence in the world, creating a larger shape and gaining muscle. Despite these apparent differences, both conditions involve complex interrelated pressures about appearance, the ideal body, individual perception and self-esteem.

BINGE-EATING DISORDER (BED)

BED is characterized by recurrent and persistent 'binge' episodes displaying the following features: eating much more rapidly than normal, eating until feeling uncomfortably full, eating large amounts of food when not physically hungry, eating alone because of embarrassment at the amount of food one is eating, and experiencing self-disgust, depression or extreme guilt after bingeing. There is a loss of control (or a sense of being out of control) during these episodes. The person will usually eat very quickly and often in secret. Individuals with BED may also stockpile food to consume secretly at a later time. They often eat normally with others but binge when alone. They experience anxiety that can only be relieved by eating, although they do not actually reach satiation, and they often experience numbness or lack of sensation while bingeing.

BED was included in the latest (5th) edition of the DSM (see **DSM**). In previous editions, it was relegated to an Appendix and many experts included it under the catch-all term 'eating disorders not otherwise specified' (see **EATING DISORDERS NOT OTHERWISE SPECIFIED**). The recognition since of BED as a distinct eating disorder in its own right is important in terms of diagnosis and treatment, as well as for those individuals who have this highly distressing condition. Like anorexia, BED has long been misunderstood, with the main focus being on the large quantities of food consumed and resulting weight problems. BED's inclusion as an official mental disorder opens up the way for a deeper understanding of this complex condition.

While obesity is an increasing health problem across Western countries, binge-eating is more complicated than just overeating. Binge-eating is not just having the occasional large meal or an overindulgent weekend. According to the online support group BEDA, BED is now the most common form of disordered eating in the USA, affecting three times as many people as anorexia and bulimia combined. Binge-eating differs from overeating in the quantity of food consumed and the frequency and psychological distress caused by the behaviour. Unlike bulimics, binge-eaters do not usually compensate by vomiting or over-exercising. A typical binge is followed by feelings of intense shame, guilt or self-disgust.

Binge-eating is an expensive and uncomfortable habit to maintain, inducing both physical and psychological distress. The frequency of binges may vary from daily to a few times a month. Whereas an average binge can consist of several thousand calories, a severe binge can involve consuming up to 30,000 calories in a single sitting: this is around two weeks' worth of food for the average adult. Individuals may visit many different shops to avoid detection or adverse comments.

Binge foods are usually high in sugar, fat and carbohydrates. Biscuits, bread, cake, ice-cream, pizza and crisps are typical. This high-calorie food is often consumed at great speed in a kind of trance or stupor – people report not even tasting the food as it goes down. Binges are also characterized by unusual combinations of food: a jar of lemon curd, fish fingers and chocolate cake, for example. The person focuses more on rapid consumption than on enjoyment or flavour. Some people say they feel that they are trying to make themselves 'explode'. Like individuals with anorexia, they may hear a 'voice' telling them to eat more and more; like anorexics, they are secretive about their behaviour. They conceal empty packets inside other packets or eat in the car, in the middle of the night or plan binges when alone.

Although most people with obesity do not have BED, up to two-thirds of people with BED are obese and experience the medical complications associated with this condition. They also display higher levels of anxiety and depression than control groups of obese people who do not binge, and normal-weight people. Clearly, binge-eating can be extremely dangerous to an individual's physical health, with risks including cardiovascular disease, type 2 diabetes, hypertension, muscle and joint pain, and gallbladder and gastrointestinal complications.

Binge-eating also affects individuals' emotional well-being. They may become socially isolated and depressed, even suicidal. Binge-eating can affect anyone, male or female, of any age. The condition is still widely misunderstood and carries social stigma, with people being shouted at in public places, told to 'just stop eating' or get some willpower. (See also **MYTHS AND MISUNDERSTANDINGS**.)

Like anorexia and bulimia, the roots of BED often lie in early experiences of insecurity, rejection or fear. When a child is not able to rely on emotional support, it makes sense that he or she will turn elsewhere for reassurance. Difficult emotions are buried under the routine of 'comfort' eating instead, and the behaviour becomes habitual.

Awareness among the medical community is slowly improving, but specific treatment for BED remains limited: most eating disorder services in the UK focus on anorexia and bulimia. Professional support from psychiatrists, nutritionists and therapists is essential for addressing these distressing and destructive eating habits.

CBT has been shown to be highly effective in the treatment of BED. Compared with waiting list patients, people with BED who received CBT showed significant reductions in body mass index (BMI), in the number of days a binge occurred, and in disinhibition, hunger, depression and low self-esteem. Those who had CBT were also more likely to be free from binge-eating at the end of treatment.

Dialectical behaviour therapy, another form of talking treatment that was originally developed to help those with borderline personality disorders, can provide practical strategies to cope with stress, regulate emotions, and minimize and eventually stop binge-eating. Other forms of interpersonal group therapy and support groups can help people to feel less alone by discussing issues and sharing coping strategies, and to dispel the shame and secrecy of BED.

Individuals with BED are also more prone to alcoholism and other substance abuse. Research shows that binge-eating and binge-drinking share many common risk factors. The cycle of secretive and self-destructive behaviour, fuelled by shame and low self-esteem, is common to both bingeing on food and bingeing on alcohol. (See also **ALCOHOL**.)

BIOAVAILABILITY

Bioavailability describes how readily the body can absorb the nutrients it needs, specifically in relation to essential vitamins and minerals. For example, iron from 'haem' or meat sources is said to be more bioavailable than iron from 'non-haem' or plant-based sources. This does not mean that non-meat-eaters cannot absorb the iron they need from a vegetarian diet, but they may need to combine it with other nutrients (such as vitamin C) to optimize its absorption by the body. (See also **VEGANISM**, **VITAMIN B GROUP**, **VITAMIN K**, **SUPPLEMENTS** and **IRON**.)

BIPOLAR DISORDER

The eating disorder most commonly associated with bipolar disorder is bulimia nervosa. However, bipolar disorder is also seen in individuals who have anorexia and BED. Bipolar disorder differs from major depression in that it has two 'poles' – hence 'bipolar' – and oscillates between extreme highs and lows. Individuals with bipolar disorder may sink into a deep depression lasting several days or weeks. At other times, they develop a euphoric or manic mood elevation, hence the old-fashioned term 'manic-depressive' illness.

While the depressive aspects of bipolar disorder can be crippling for the person, the manic side also causes problems – that is, the highs can be as perilous as the lows. When manic, individuals may experience unlimited enthusiasm and optimism, throwing themselves into new projects, spending money, socializing or exercising to dangerous excess, believing they can achieve anything and harming themselves in the process. During manic episodes, people with bipolar disorder often have no insight into their condition; the sense of creativity and invincibility can cause problems in their careers, personal relationships and finances, and may put them physically at risk. The flip side of these euphoric episodes is the periods of extreme lows, when individuals' self-confidence and positivity evaporate, they despair and may even become suicidally depressed.

Individuals with bipolar disorder often struggle with eating disorders too. The rapid mood fluctuations symptomatic of bipolar disorder can be significantly worsened by erratic eating patterns and cycles of bingeing and purging. It is not clear exactly why bipolar disorder should be linked with eating disorders (especially bulimia), but they share many characteristics, including eating irregularities, weight problems, poor impulse control, self-destructive habits, compulsive behaviours and repeating certain acts or rituals according to certain rules (similar to OCD). Eating disorders and bipolar disorder also share a tendency to 'cycle': between bulimia and anorexia, and between depression and mania.

Bipolar disorder sounds alarming to those who do not understand it and still carries an unfortunate social stigma, even though it is not really rare: approximately 0.5–1 per cent of the adult population are thought to have it and many more experience major depressive episodes. There is growing evidence that bipolar disorder may run in families. As research has developed, treatment has improved, with medication such as lithium often proving helpful in stabilizing neurochemical imbalances. Talking therapies, and a good relationship with a counsellor, can significantly improve an individual's experience.

Managing bipolar disorder *and* an eating disorder can be challenging. For example, some antidepressants used to treat eating disorders can trigger a manic mood swing in people with bipolar disorder. Conversely, some mood stabilizers or antipsychotics used to treat bipolar disorder have been known to trigger binge-eating episodes. The severity of a person's bipolar disorder is likely to have an influence on the severity of the eating disorder, and vice versa. Recovery depends on both conditions being properly diagnosed.

Cyclothymia is a milder form of bipolar disorder also common in eating-disordered individuals (see **CYCLOTHYMIA**).

BODY DYSMORPHIC DISORDER (BDD)

This describes an extreme preoccupation with one or more features of one's own body that are not particularly noticeable or abnormal to others. Individuals with BDD are usually very self-conscious; they may describe themselves as 'ugly' or 'different' and experience a feeling of not being 'right'. They often compulsively check their appearance in the mirror, never satisfied with what they see. In severe cases of BDD, individuals may undergo unnecessary and repeated cosmetic or dermatological procedures, which rarely resolve the psychological problem.

Symptoms of BDD range widely and include compulsive skin-picking, trichotillomania (where a person feels compelled to pull their hair out), anorexia, bulimia, depression, social phobias and anxiety disorders. It is a complex condition; those who look 'normal' may be affected, while those with actual physical disfigurements such as burns or scars may not.

Up to 1 per cent of the world's population are thought to have BDD, and it is more prevalent in cultures where cosmetic surgery is common and in societies where appearance is highly valued. As every person is individual, it is impossible to find a single cause for BDD and body-image issues. There are some obvious triggers, such as being teased or bullied in adolescence, but other factors also make the individual more vulnerable, such as childhood abuse or trauma. Having a family history of mental illness appears to contribute, as does the culture and environment in which you grow up, your own personality and other psychological and neurological traits.

BDD is not solely linked to body size, shape and weight: the most common concern is with the skin, especially problems such as acne or eczema, followed by concerns about facial features such as the nose, chin, lips or eyes. People complain about a lack of symmetry, often feeling that specific features or parts of their body are too large, too small or out of proportion.

Both sexes are equally affected by BDD, although women and men tend to focus on different parts of their body. Women are more likely to be preoccupied with breasts, hips, weight and legs, whereas men tend to be preoccupied with body build (see **BIGOREXIA**). Men are also more likely to report concerns over their genitals, usually that their penis is too small, or concerns that their chest and torso are not masculine enough.

BDD usually begins in adolescence, a period of significant physical changes, with sexual development, hormonal changes and what can be quite significant growth spurts, affecting height and weight. It's also the period when people are most sensitive about their appearance, and most concerned about being physically attractive to their peers.

Secrecy and shame are a large part of BDD. Many people hide their problems for many years or never seek help as they feel ashamed of their feelings. Not only do they dislike their appearance, but they also fear being labelled as vain or narcissistic. Just as anorexia is easily confused with wanting to be thin and beautiful, BDD is easily confused with vanity. In fact, the opposite is true: people with BDD want to fit in, not stand out.

The degree of impairment in BDD varies from mild to severe. While some people are able to keep their disorder mostly hidden, others find it affects relationships, work, social interactions and every area of their lives. Even in its mildest form, however, BDD causes emotional or mental distress. You might avoid social activities you have previously enjoyed and become withdrawn. You might spend more time alone, in bed or avoid seeing friends. You might use alcohol or drugs to numb your feelings or ruminate on unpleasant or upsetting things that have happened. You might experience humiliation or rejection, blaming any failures or setbacks in your life on your supposed physical abnormalities.

In the past, BDD has been portrayed as a kind of 'imagined ugliness', as if people were wildly delusional. However, people with milder BDD often have a good insight into their condition. They are aware that their feelings about their appearance may be unfounded or irrational – but they are still unable to control them. At the more severe end of the spectrum, people may be convinced of their supposed abnormality. To them, their physical defects are a reality, no matter how many times other people reassure them that they look normal.

Although research into BDD is nowhere near as advanced as research into depression and other mental illnesses, things are changing. As more trials are being carried out into different psychological therapies and medication, doctors and therapists are starting to develop effective guidelines and treatment. The experience of individuals (in books, blogs and articles) also provides valuable evidence of the causes and consequences of mild, moderate and severe forms of BDD, and how they respond to treatment. The evidence indicates that BDD *is* treatable, and people can get back to a normal life. Whether this involves self-help, CBT, anti-obsessional medication or a combination of all three, BDD is not a life sentence.

People with BDD are often also very depressed, and sadly have a high rate of attempted suicide. BDD is more common than we might think, and nothing to be ashamed of: the most important first step is to speak to someone, and to seek help from mental health professionals.

BODY IMAGE

This describes our internalized sense of what we look like, the picture we hold in our minds of the size, weight and shape of our own body. This mental representation is made up of various factors, including mirror image, photographs we see of ourselves, how we think we look in the eyes of observers, idealized images of how we would like to look, the feedback we receive from others, and our general sense of worth and self-esteem.

The term 'body image' is widely used in magazines, on TV, in casual conversations and in everyday life, but it stands for a complex set of self-beliefs, attitudes and perceptions. It involves deeply personal issues of body ownership and identity, how we feel we look and how we judge ourselves. Body image also describes our attitudes towards the constituent parts of our body: which bits do we focus on, what do we criticize or wish we could change? (See also **LANGUAGE**.)

Body image is multidimensional, formed through a range of interrelated factors: activity in our brain's somatosensory cortex, but also endless input from the world around us. Body image may or may not be stable: it may change over time, for example from adolescence to middle age, and for women during and after pregnancy, and after the menopause. Social and cultural standards change too, with expectations for body shape constantly shifting with the fashions, from boyish androgyny to hourglass curvy.

Body image can be affected from day to day by mood and by hormones (especially in women) and even by simple factors such as what we're wearing: tighter or looser clothes affect people's perception of their own size. Body image can be affected by what we've eaten, what others do and say, and how we perceive they act towards us. Stepping on the bathroom scales can have a positive or negative impact on body image (see **SCALES**), as can looking at images of ourselves and others, online, on social media or in magazines.

Not everyone responds to different *parts* of their body in the same way. We tend to be good at responding to temperature by, for example, putting on or taking off a jumper, or at responding to thirst by drinking a glass of water. However, hunger is far more complicated, and those with eating disorders display real difficulty in responding to this simple physiological need (see **DEPRIVATION**).

Nor do we judge all parts of our body in the same way: women often express far more emotional or critical responses to specific aspects of their bodies, usually those associated with sexual attractiveness. They feel that their breasts or bottoms, for example, are too big or too small, whereas they rarely say the same about their hands or feet. Interestingly, the areas of the body most commonly misrepresented among people with eating disorders are their hips, thighs and torso.

Body-image disturbance is a core symptom of eating disorders. We have seen that, due to cultural and social factors, and the Western concept of the 'perfect body', almost all women (and many men) express dissatisfaction with their body weight and shape. However, research shows that in eating disorders, disturbed body image is significantly different from that seen in the general population.

Some degree of body-image disturbance is common – in studies, patients with anorexia generally overestimate their body size more than healthy controls – but this varies widely. One of the myths and misunderstandings of anorexia is that all people have wildly distorted body image: the anorexic stereotype shows an *emaciated* woman looking in the mirror seeing an *obese* woman looking back. This is not always the case. Some anorexics have considerable insight into their physical condition and can clearly see how underweight they are. Others may genuinely see fat where others see skin and bone.

Body image, therefore, isn't just about what you see: it's about how you feel in your own skin. The paradox in severe eating disorders is how persistent the perceptions and beliefs around body image can be, despite the facts. For example, someone with severe anorexia can be confronted with the evidence: their weight is much lower than that of the general population. They have to buy the smallest size of clothing in the shops. They are unable to eat a normal meal like others do. They are causing intense anxiety to their family, friends and doctors; they may even be in hospital.

These individuals are often highly intelligent, and yet in some way their mental image of their body is stronger than the facts. They have a persistent experience of feeling fat even when all the evidence proves that they are extremely underweight. They are often unable to accept that they are dangerously malnourished, because the feeling of being fat or greedy overrides the medical or visual reality. However, research into neuroscience and body-image perception has found that anorexic individuals tended only to overestimate their own body size, not the sizes of other bodies or neutral objects, which suggests that body image and self-perception are complicated issues – for both healthy individuals who are eating, and those who are not.

The influence of cultural factors, especially the thin body ideal of Western society and the growth of social media, has contributed to increasingly unstable or negative body image. An NHS study in 2016 reported that mental illness among young women was soaring, with anxiety, depression, self-harm and eating disorders all on the increase. Young women have become a 'key high-risk group', with 1 in 5 women, compared with 1 in 8 men, having a mental illness. It is notable that rates of serious mental illness have remained largely unchanged among men for the years during which they have been rising among women.

Along with individual reasons such as childhood trauma and sexual abuse, social media has been identified as one of the major contributors to increased mental illness. Social media exerts pressure on young people to look a certain way, presenting them with unrealistic expectations and airbrushed images of physical perfection. With or without the physical and psychological impact of eating disorders, many individuals are familiar with the daily body-image struggle: how they feel and how they think they ought to look.

Neuroscientific research has not yet located a specific area in the brain associated with the body-image disturbance seen in eating disorders. Indeed, it is unlikely that there is one single region or pathway that determines an individual's body image, although the insula is of great interest to scientists (see **INSULA**). Research has, however, highlighted the complicated and interrelated factors involved in the simple experience of being inside one's own body.

Mood and hormones play a role, as do outside social and cultural influences, as do a person's temperament and other random factors. Aggravating aspects of eating disorders such as prolonged restriction, extreme low weight, substance abuse, purging, and neurochemical imbalances associated with bingeing and purging, make the situation even more complicated. Neuroimaging studies have highlighted similar neural patterns in anorexia and bulimia, suggesting that brain processes involved in body-image disturbance in the two conditions are closer than it might appear. As ever in eating disorders research, it is unclear whether neural differences are a cause or a consequence of starvation.

As a first step, however, it is important to remember that feelings are not facts: body image isn't always reliable. For everyone, it's a deeply personal interaction between the inner world and external reality, psychological and sociocultural factors. In those with eating disorders, body image tends to become more positive as other symptoms improve: a more stable eating pattern and improved nutrition lifts the mood and bolsters self-esteem.

BODY MASS INDEX (BMI)

BMI is calculated by dividing weight in kilograms (kg) by the square of the height in metres. A BMI above 25 is defined as overweight and above 30 is defined as obese. Although the BMI calculation gives an accurate guide to an individual's weight to height ratio, it fails to take into account different body shapes or composition.

In recent years, some experts have discredited the standard BMI measurement as a blunt instrument because it takes no account of the fact that abdominal fat, the so-called 'apple shape', tends to be more dangerous than fat around the bottom and thighs, the 'pear shape'. Nor does BMI take into account the fact that healthy muscle weighs more than unhealthy fat. For example, even though many bodybuilders have only 10 per cent body fat, a BMI calculator would give them an 'overweight' result. For the same reason, some elite athletes would also be classified as overweight when they are clearly not. Another measurement, known as ABSI (A Body Shape Index) and which combines BMI and waist circumference, has been introduced as a possible alternative to BMI. (See also **SCALES**.)

BOREDOM

It may seem surprising to include boredom in an A to Z of eating disorders, but many people find that boredom is their main trigger for overeating. This is part of the obesogenic society in which we live: opportunities for eating are everywhere, simply to pass the time, such as in airports, shopping centres or cinemas. As a result, we find ourselves buying and consuming food that we are not really hungry for. When constant snacking becomes a habit or a way to fill the time, we can lose the ability to identify what genuine hunger feels like.

The solution to boredom snacking, of course, is to get busy! When you're studying, working, interested or absorbed, rushing around with no time to spare, you're unlikely to consume excessive quantities of unhealthy snacks. Although there is nothing wrong with the occasional indulgence or just enjoying cake and coffee with a friend, in general food should be fuel. Food should be consumed *mindfully* not *mindlessly* (see **MINDFUL EATING**). Instead of grazing in front of the TV, at the cinema, when hanging around at the airport, we should try to sit down to a meal three times a day. This is not always possible during a busy working day, but it's always possible to give a few minutes to focus on the food in front of us, even if it's just a sandwich at your desk. Finding different ways to respond to boredom is essential: a walk in the fresh air, writing a page or two of a journal, ringing a friend. This will break the association between food and boredom and help to re-establish the link between hunger and eating. (See also **EMOTIONAL EATING**.)

BRAIN

The brain is a hungry organ, and in order to function properly it needs regular, good-quality fuel. Although the brain makes up only 2 per cent of total body weight, it uses 20 per cent of the body's energy supplies. Brain cells need high-energy foods because every cell connects and communicates with thousands of other cells. When calories are severely restricted, as in anorexia, the brain struggles to function. This causes cognitive impairment, including impaired memory, concentration, learning, studying and creative thinking. In semi-starvation, all the brain's normal functions are affected.

The root of the neuroscientific approach to eating disorders is that starving the body also starves the brain. As neuroscience has developed in recent decades, the understanding of anorexia nervosa has progressed rapidly. Most clinicians, psychiatrists and neuroscientists would now agree that there are significant genetic and neurological factors involved in anorexia. Whether the identifiable differences in brain structure – such as the shrunken insula and thalamus – are caused by pre-existing factors or caused or exacerbated by starvation is not known. However, it is clear that anorexia shows many markers of being a brain disease rather than simply a lifestyle choice, food phobia or loss of hunger.

BULIMAREXIA

This is a portmanteau word describing the combination of both bulimia and anorexic symptoms. Few individuals with an eating disorder will fit neatly into a single category of only restricting or only binge-purging. Instead most people alternate between episodes of restriction and episodes of binge-purging, although one behaviour is usually more dominant. The cyclical nature of disordered eating means that self-starvation is likely to lead to overeating, which is likely to lead to purging, hence the common syndrome of bulimarexia, where several different characteristics are present.

BULIMIA NERVOSA

The original root of this is the Greek word *boulimia*, meaning 'hunger like an ox'. As with the literal meaning of anorexia, this definition is misleading (and possibly offensive). Those who have bulimia do not 'hunger like an ox': they have simply developed disordered behaviours in relation to food.

Bulimia is characterized by recurrent episodes of binge-eating (see **BINGE-EATING DISORDER**) but with self-induced vomiting, laxative and diuretic abuse, and other compensatory behaviours to avoid weight gain. In the latest edition of the DSM (5th edition, 2013), requirements for diagnosing bulimia nervosa were changed from 'at least twice weekly for 6 months' to 'at least once weekly over the last 3 months'.

As in anorexia, shape and weight are core preoccupations in bulimia, and people tend to overestimate their own body shape and weight. Bulimia can be more difficult to detect than anorexia because people tend to be of average, or only slightly above/below average, weight. Unlike anorexia, therefore, the physical signs of bulimia are not immediately visible.

Like the hungry 'high' that many anorexics experience in prolonged starvation, bulimia can become addictive, behaviourally but also chemically. Both bingeing and vomiting can trigger waves of endorphins, potent 'feel-good' brain chemicals. The release of these natural heroin-like chemicals reinforces the powerful compulsion to purge, which bulimics often feel helpless to fight. For outsiders, who associate vomiting with feeling very unwell, this is incomprehensible. Everything about vomiting appears to be unpleasant, so bulimia is deeply misunderstood.

In fact, bulimia is surprisingly common, although exact figures are impossible to come by, because of the hidden nature of the condition. Studies at American high schools and colleges have reported that from 60 to 80 per cent of the female students binge, purge and starve on a regular basis. Girls reported that skipping meals turns into all-day fasting, followed by 'pig-outs' when the hunger becomes unbearable, after which vomiting, laxatives or diet pills are used.

C

CALCIUM

Calcium is the most abundant mineral in the human body. Its primary function is to build and maintain healthy bones and teeth. It also regulates muscle contractions, including the heartbeat, and ensures that blood clots normally. Around 90 per cent of the body's calcium is in our bones.

When there is insufficient calcium for normal biological functioning, stored calcium is used instead. This can seriously deplete bone mass and lead to brittle bones, fractures and breakages. Fragile and porous bones and its precursor osteopenia (see **OSTEOPOROSIS/ OSTEOPENIA**) are serious conditions. As vitamin D is essential for calcium absorption, it's important to get enough vitamin D through regular exposure of the skin to daylight (at least 15 minutes a day) and through adequate dietary intake.

Bones increase in size and mass up to the age of around 30, so it is crucial to obtain adequate calcium (and vitamin D) in childhood and adolescence, especially for girls and women. Insufficient calcium is extremely common in young women who are restricting calories, avoiding dairy products and fat, and are missing periods. It should be noted here that low-fat dairy options contain the same amount of calcium as the corresponding full-fat products, so they are good sources of calcium.

Adults need around 700 mg of calcium a day. Women who are breastfeeding or postmenopausal need more. Milk, yogurt and cheese are rich natural sources of calcium. Non-dairy sources include green leafy vegetables such as kale, broccoli and cabbage. Soya, tofu, nuts and fish with bones (such as pilchards and sardines) are also good sources of calcium. Other strategies for healthy levels of calcium include not smoking, and taking regular weight-bearing activity (such as walking or running) to keep the bones strong.

As well as being crucial for bone health, calcium plays a central role in neuronal activity: almost every neurochemical signal in our brains involves calcium. When too much calcium is released, as in the bone loss seen in anorexia, this may lead to brain cell loss.

CARBOHYDRATES

The human body is designed to run on carbohydrates. While protein and fat also provide energy, carbohydrates are the easiest and most immediate source of fuel.

Carbohydrates can be particularly problematic for individuals with eating disorders. In anorexia, the person tends to avoid 'bulky' carbohydrate foods, such as bread and pasta, in the mistaken belief that these will make them fat. In reality, they need these carbs for a wide range of body functions, from concentrating to staying warm, moving around and maintaining stable moods and good digestive and bowel functioning. Carbohydrates control our blood sugar, which in turn controls our appetite and weight and metabolism.

Carbohydrates can also be problematic in bulimia and binge-eating. Most 'binge' foods are carbohydrate-heavy and of the simple, sugary variety rather than complex, slow-release carbs. As we will see, consuming large quantities of simple carbs only worsens the inevitable blood sugar imbalance. During a binge, the body experiences a rapid increase in blood sugar levels, followed soon after by a crash (and purging only worsens this yo-yo cycle), but cutting out carbohydrates is not the answer: everyone, whatever their weight, benefits from a steady release of energy from 'good' carbs. In order to understand which carbohydrates to choose, we need to differentiate between complex and simple carbohydrates.

- **Complex carbohydrates** include whole grains, pulses, lentils, beans and vegetables. The body takes longer to digest these foods, breaking down the fibres and taking the nutrients it needs. This slower digestion process releases energy slowly, keeps blood sugar levels steady and keeps you feeling fuller for longer. Complex carbs also aid the digestive process.

- **Simple carbohydrates** are refined, white or overcooked foods, such as white bread, white rice, white pasta, refined sugars such as glucose, honey and syrup, dried fruit and sweets. Refined carbs act like refined sugars: the process of refining or cooking foods starts the process of breaking down complex carbs into simple carbs, effectively pre-digesting them. This means that the sugar is rapidly absorbed, causing a spike in blood sugar and energy levels. Fruit admittedly contains simple sugars, but in many fruits this is fructose rather than glucose. The body has to convert this fructose into glucose, for use in cells, which slows down the energy-release process. Grapes and dates contain glucose (and are therefore simple, fast-release carbs), whereas apples contain fructose (and are therefore much slower-release).

In general, there are a lot of tempting, simple carbohydrates around: cakes, biscuits, chocolate bars, sweets, white bread, pasta, fruit juices, most breakfast cereals and many other artificially sweetened substances. In fact, sugar consumption in Western diets is excessive: we could all benefit from fewer simple carbs and more complex ones. Endurance athletes may need this immediate, abundant energy but most of us don't, and when sugar is not required as fuel, it is stored as fat. Sugar is also low on nutrients (around 90 per cent of the vitamins and minerals have been removed from white sugar) so sugary simple carbohydrates are empty calories.

Conversely, complex carbohydrates not only provide our bodies with an excellent, steady source of fuel, they are also essential for healthy brain functioning. Restricting carbohydrates leads to depleted levels of the mood regulator serotonin. Individuals on extreme low-carbohydrate regimes often become very depressed. Lack of carbohydrates also risks exacerbating anxiety and OCD (see **ANXIETY** and **OBSESSIVE COMPULSIVE DISORDER**).

CARBOHYDRATES

There has been an explosion of low-carb eating in recent years, such as the Atkins and Dukan diets, with their severely restricted carbohydrate content. While these diets appear to show rapid results, any weight loss is mostly short-lived, and is caused by dehydration and water loss rather than an actual decrease in body weight. Additionally, these low- or no-carb diets often ration fruit and vegetables (which contain essential vitamins and minerals) and substitute carbs with excessive fat: bacon, eggs, cream, butter and so on. Clearly, this kind of unbalanced eating is unwise: it's just as unhealthy to consume too few carbs as too many. Extreme low-carbohydrate diets also create a sense of deprivation: Atkins dieters often report cravings for bread, pasta, potatoes and other forbidden carbohydrates. Eliminating entire food groups can be a trigger for binge-eating and bulimia, where the craving for 'bad' food gets out of control, and the individual just crams it all in. (See also **BINGE-EATING DISORDER, DEPRIVATION, SEROTONIN** and **ANXIETY**.)

CARDIAC COMPLICATIONS

Repeated bingeing and purging place the body under extreme stress, and can lead to cardiac arrest and sudden death. Prolonged laxative or emetic abuse can also damage the heart. Sadly, cardiac abnormalities are a leading cause of death in individuals with anorexia or bulimia. The combination of prolonged starvation and electrolyte disturbance (see **ELECTROLYTES**) causes irregularities in the heartbeat. Anorexia also causes a potentially fatal slowing down of the electrical impulses that regulate a normal heartbeat; this slowing can lead to serious cardiac arrhythmia.

Intense exercise exerts yet more stress on the heart. As well as having a low heart rate (bradycardia), individuals who are starving may have abnormally low blood pressure (hypotension). They may experience dizziness or fainting on standing, swelling in the feet and ankles or a blue tinge to the feet and hands (called cyanosis) due to problems with their circulatory system and impaired temperature regulation.

Warning signs such as palpitations – rapid or irregular heartbeat – dizziness, tingling or blackouts can indicate serious cardiac problems. Anyone who experiences these symptoms should seek medical help immediately. Cardiac irregularities can be detected by a heart monitor, known as an electrocardiograph (ECG).

CHILDHOOD DISORDERS

Unlike adolescent or adult-onset conditions, eating disorders in childhood do not appear to be driven primarily by concern over body weight or shape. Research into the clinical and psychiatric features of disordered eating in childhood is still relatively limited. It is, however, clear that problems tend to involve dysfunctional behaviour around food, irregular or inadequate food intake, avoidance of eating or fear of swallowing or choking. Eating disorders in childhood are rare, but some of the main conditions are food-avoidance emotional disorder, selective eating and functional dysphagia.

FOOD-AVOIDANCE EMOTIONAL DISORDER

It's still unclear whether this is primarily an emotional/mood disorder or an eating disorder. Children with this condition display symptoms similar to anorexia nervosa: they are usually very underweight and restrict their food intake. In small studies, the ratio of food-avoidance emotional disorder in girls to boys was 4:1.

SELECTIVE EATING

These children typically eat a very narrow range of foods for at least 2 years, and are unwilling or unable to try new foods. Unlike anorexia or bulimia, they display no preoccupation with weight or shape. Selective eating is often described as a developmental, or even a phobic, disorder. Preferred or 'safe' foods in selective eating are often soft carbohydrate-based foods, such as white bread, pasta or chips. There are a wide range of reasons for selective eating depending on the child's own experiences, including problems with using cutlery, delayed chewing skills or sensory sensitivity. Most cases of selective eating tend to resolve with age. Compared with food-avoidance emotional disorder, the ratio of selective eating is reversed, being 4:1 in boys to girls.

FUNCTIONAL DYSPHAGIA

This is a fear of swallowing, vomiting or choking. There is usually an identifiable trigger for the fear, such as the child having choked on a piece of food or having had distressing gastrointestinal problems, or there may be some other trauma associated with specific tastes or textures. The result is an anxiety around food and avoidance of eating. Dysphagia may be seen alongside other childhood eating disorders.

CHILDREN

Early-onset eating disorders (that is, arising before puberty) are relatively rare, but their incidence does appear to be increasing. The damage from a childhood eating disorder, in physical, social, educational and emotional terms, can be even more severe than eating disorders in adolescents and adults, for several reasons.

The physical deterioration seen in eating disorders tends to be more marked in children. This is due to smaller fat reserves in their bodies and rapid changes in their size and growth. If a condition like anorexia occurs before puberty, sexual maturation is often delayed and the delay may be permanent (see **AMENORRHOEA**). Growth impairment can have permanent effects on adult stature. If a child is severely undernourished during childhood and adolescence, it is harder to make up the lost growth. Children are smaller and less robust, and therefore more susceptible to dehydration and starvation, than adults. For the same reason, vomiting and diuretic and laxative abuse are dangerous in children. The bone-thinning condition known as osteoporosis is also more serious in children, especially girls. Childhood, adolescence and the early twenties are a crucial time for laying down bone mass (to last the rest of our lives). When the disorder starts before bones are fully mineralized, normal peak bone mass is never achieved. This can result in stunting and deformity, as well as frequent bone fractures or breakages.

Finally, the social and psychological complications are serious in early-onset eating disorders, since childhood is the time when we normally learn to make friends and form relationships, study and develop personal interests and abilities. This natural process of development is disrupted when a child is very sick, spending a lot of time in hospital, detached from peers, missing school or simply depressed, anxious and hungry. It also exerts a heavy toll on the family, and may affect his or her siblings.

CLEAN EATING

This aspirational diet and lifestyle movement, driven by social media, has gained considerable popularity in recent years. It has also attracted widespread criticism from scientists and nutritionists for its unfounded claims and unscientific basis.

'Clean eating' describes a diet free of perceived 'bad' stuff, whether that's gluten, grains or dairy, and may even advocate the cutting out of entire food groups. It involves a strict avoidance of 'processed' substances such as caffeine, alcohol, sugar or wheat, common preservatives and other so-called 'chemicals'. However, every atom in the universe is a 'chemical' – water is a chemical, every cell in our bodies is a chemical; no single substance is inherently solely 'good' or 'bad'.

'Clean eating', like 'superfoods', is a pseudoscientific term that labels some food as purer, more virtuous – literally 'cleaner' – than other foods. Clean eaters talk of 'real' food, 'in its most natural state', and claim that 'eating clean' can transform your health. There are even stories of miraculous recovery from illnesses as serious as cancer. The movement has been fuelled by a generation of photogenic young bloggers and YouTubers, mostly female, with sketchy nutritional qualifications, and often with cookery books, TV shows or fitness regimes to promote.

Clean eating differs from other diets in that it's an aspirational, lifestyle movement, fuelled by motivational hashtags, digitally perfected images of natural beauty and extreme physical fitness, and a moral/spiritual dimension.

The core principles of clean eating can appear fairly arbitrary: there may be intermittent fasting or 30-day juice cleanses or not eating after 6 p.m. Clean eating advocates may eat only raw, fermented or sprouted food; they may ingest clay to purify their insides. While some are strict vegans, others rhapsodize about bone broth, boiling up bones for the 'ultimate superfood'. Clean eaters are often anti-wheat and grain-free evangelists.

Like other forms of disordered eating, clean eating is an expensive habit. Its recipes typically require expensive, organic, hard-to-find ingredients and can be time-consuming to prepare. Complicated recipes may demand the endless juicing of organic fruit and vegetables, spiralizing courgettes in place of spaghetti, for example, or shopping for pricey powders and seeds to replace normal staples such as bread or milk.

Respected nutritionists agree that clean eating rules have no basis in fact, and can in reality result in a seriously restrictive diet. Avoiding dairy, for example, can contribute to calcium deficiency, which is particularly serious in young women (see **OSTEOPOROSIS/ OSTEOPENIA**). UK sales of almond milk have increased around 80 per cent year on year, but plant-based milks (such as coconut, cashew, rice or oat milk) are poor sources of protein and calcium, and often contain sweeteners to improve the taste. Soya milk provides adequate protein, but coconut milk contains more fat than full-fat cow's milk. These popular dairy alternatives are not all they seem – plant milks have been described as 'creamy low-protein high-carbohydrate sugar-sweetened soft drinks'.

Clean eating looks beautiful on Instagram, but it can be as restrictive, time-consuming and obsessive as **ORTHOREXIA**, fuelling the kind of food anxiety that can lead to seriously disordered eating. It's a perfect storm of extreme calorie restriction, avoidance and fear of a wide range of foods, excessive exercise and an intense focus on the body. It plays on the modern uncertainty and paranoia about where our food comes from, and combines neurotic eating, body dysmorphia and obsessive behaviour. Unsurprisingly, clean eating is often a gateway to more severe eating disorders.

COGNITIVE BEHAVIOURAL THERAPY (CBT)

Originally known as cognitive therapy, this popular talking therapy now incorporates behavioural principles. The technique was developed by the psychiatrist and psychoanalyst Aaron Beck in the early 1960s. When treating depressed patients, Beck noticed that their negative cognitions, which he called 'automatic thoughts', fell into three categories: negative ideas about the self, the world and the future.

The principle behind CBT is simple: our thoughts directly affect our feelings, which in turn affect how we behave. When we recognize negative thoughts as they arise, we can challenge them and learn how to reframe them. In CBT, we recognize specific triggers or situations that cause our own negative thoughts, for example 'I'll always be a failure' or 'No one will ever love me.' CBT trains us to challenge these automatic negative beliefs, which many of us hold, getting us each to ask ourselves, 'What is the evidence that I will always be a failure? Where is the proof that I'm unlovable?'

Once we question these beliefs, we can see that they are not based on reality or are outdated or downright wrong. Failing to get a promotion once or experiencing a relationship breakdown in the past does not mean that we are destined to repeat this for ever. CBT helps us to replace irrational automatic thoughts with more positive, realistic versions, and thus to function more healthily. It can help us challenge ourselves – and 'change the record'. CBT is now routinely offered by the NHS for depression, stress, phobias and many anxiety disorders, including OCD.

Individuals with anorexia nervosa often have a negative internal mindset, with repetitive thoughts structured around fear and failure. They set themselves impossibly high standards, and always compare up rather than down. They may have rigid thinking styles, which causes them to overreact to small comments or events, and they are often unable to see the bigger picture (see **COGNITIVE IMPAIRMENT**). Things are either amazing or disastrous, with little in between. Perfectionism, hopelessness, self-blame and guilt tend to fuel the negativity. Individuals' thoughts usually focus on the body, food habits and eating behaviours: thoughts such as, 'I've always been greedy, I'll never get my bingeing under control' in bulimia or, 'I'm worthless, I don't deserve to eat' in anorexia. In almost all cases of anorexia, the less the person eats, the more rigid and 'stuck' their negative automatic thoughts become.

CBT helps to distinguish facts from feelings. Emotions and reality are different things, and CBT helps us get some distance on intense feelings that are not actually real. A trained CBT therapist will guide you through the confusion of negative automatic thoughts, and give you a more objective perspective on the situation. He or she will also suggest relaxation exercises to counteract severe and pervasive anxiety. CBT can be an effective way of challenging the repetitive distorted thoughts, thus helping the person to break free of the cycle of disordered eating. (See also **COGNITIVE REMEDIATION THERAPY, COPING STRATEGIES** and **SELF-COMPASSION**.)

COGNITIVE IMPAIRMENT

The brain needs a steady supply of fuel for optimal functioning, and when it's inadequately or irregularly fed, it will struggle. As well as the external physical damage they cause, eating disorders cause significant difficulties inside the head. Concentrating, learning, remembering, considering, assessing, deciding, communicating – all these essential cognitive processes are disrupted when food is in short supply.

Individuals with eating disorders display a range of cognitive impairments. They may struggle with 'set-shifting', the ability to switch between mental sets either behaviourally or cognitively. Instead individuals with anorexia display a form of cognitive rigidity in which they find it hard to think flexibly or see things from alternative points of view. Individuals (and those close to them) report an all-or-nothing mindset, where things are either fantastic or disastrous. When trying to think around a problem, they appear very rigid; they cannot see the wood for the trees. This is also known as central coherence: the processing of information in terms of the whole picture, as well as the fine detail. Individuals often focus on the fine detail, which leads to a preoccupation with minutiae, order and symmetry, at the expense of the context.

These deficits in central coherence and 'set-shifting' have been picked up in neuropsychological research, talking to individuals and setting tasks, as well as in neuroimaging studies (see **NEUROSCIENCE**). Impaired set-shifting or central coherence seems to be associated with reduced activation in key brain regions of the left and right thalamus and their surrounding networks (specifically an area known as the ventral anterior cingulate-striato-thalamic loop). This explains the experience in anorexia of feeling 'stuck': no matter how much individuals understand they are unwell, no matter how much they need and want to gain weight, they are unable to eat. Furthermore, it explains the panic when confronted with food or social eating situations (see also **SEROTONIN**) and problems with regulating emotions.

Neuroscience has also explored risk and reward tasks in anorexia, and how individuals respond to positive and negative feedback. Findings reveal that those *with* (and even *after recovery from*) anorexia have trouble distinguishing positive and negative feedback, indicating an impaired ability to identify the emotional significance of a stimulus. These traits have interesting links to perfectionism and obsessionality, two other common eating-disordered traits. Impulsivity and decision-making are also affected, in cases of bulimia as well as anorexia. Individuals may overreact to minor upsets or take offence at the slightest criticism.

It should also be remembered that perfectly 'normal', non-eating-disordered, people also overreact when they are hungry (hence the neologism 'hangry'). They may become irritated or angry or burst into tears. Extreme hunger, a near-constant state for anorexics, explains a lot, even without factoring in neurological, biological or psychological factors.

It's also very time-consuming to be constantly trying not to eat, hiding or lying about food or avoiding the company of others. These strategies waste a lot of mental energy, as do obsessions and compulsions, guilt and shame. Recovering from an eating disorder frees up a lot of brainpower – to think and care and learn about other things.

COGNITIVE REMEDIATION THERAPY

This is a relatively new form of therapy within eating disorders that focuses on the *process* of thinking, rather than the *content*. Cognitive remediation therapy is based on decades of research (going back to the Second World War) into the neuroplasticity of the brain and its capacity to respond and adapt to environmental changes. It works by strengthening neural circuits and creating new ones, boosting and altering cognitive processes within the individual's brain, thus allowing new thinking styles to emerge.

It's well known that cognitive flexibility is a recurrent problem in eating disorders, particularly anorexia (see **COGNITIVE IMPAIRMENT**). Individuals tend to struggle with flexible thinking, adapting or 'set-shifting', and central coherence. So whereas CBT looks at *what* the individual is thinking, cognitive remediation therapy looks at *how*. It seeks to address thinking styles rather than the thoughts themselves: it seeks to correct or *remediate* the cognitive deficits or impairments. In this way, it gives individuals a greater awareness of their own cognitive style, and insight into where their maladaptive thoughts and behaviours might be coming from.

Cognitive remediation therapy is different from most forms of therapy for eating disorders. In therapy sessions, issues such as food, eating and weight are not discussed; instead the therapist and patient explore the thinking process itself. By encouraging self-reflection and practising a simple series of cognitive and behavioural exercises, the individual can start to try out alternative ways of thinking. In many cases, this leads to positive behavioural change in everyday life.

CO-MORBIDITY

This is a situation where one illness or condition is found alongside other conditions. For example, insomnia and anxiety are common co-morbidities, as are depression and cancer, and obesity and diabetes. Although it is likely that one condition may trigger or exacerbate another, this is not always the case. Co-morbidity implies correlation rather than causation: we know that depression doesn't cause cancer, but people who receive a serious diagnosis may well become depressed.

Co-morbidity is an important concept in the field of eating disorders. Many psychiatric, anxiety or mood disorders are seen alongside other disorders. Depression is the most common co-morbid disorder, and studies consistently report elevated rates of depression in individuals with eating disorders. Major depression has been reported to have a prevalence as high as 65 per cent in restrictive anorexia, and 71 per cent in binge–purge anorexia. Studies consistently report high rates of co-morbidity between mood disorders and anorexia, and between anorexia and OCD.

Anxiety disorders are also co-morbid with eating disorders: over 50 per cent of those with anorexia, and up to 75 per cent of those with bulimia, have at least one anxiety disorder. Social phobia and OCD are the most common anxiety disorders seen in anorexia. Research into psychiatric co-morbidity in BED is limited, but a large-scale clinical study found that nearly three-quarters (74 per cent) of participants with BED had at least one additional co-morbid psychiatric diagnosis, usually an anxiety or mood disorder or a substance-misuse disorder.

Remember, co-morbidity does not imply causation – it simply means that these disorders are commonly seen alongside other disorders. Given the anxiety, social isolation and physical complications involved in an eating disorder, it's not surprising that rates of depression should be so high.

COMPENSATORY BEHAVIOURS

These are behaviours intended to compensate for, or undo, calorie consumption. Behaviours include vigorous exercising, self-induced vomiting, taking laxatives or diuretics, as well as severely restricting calories or fasting to make up for eating. Compensatory behaviours have both physical and emotional dimensions. First, the individuals concerned are trying to rid themselves of, or work off, the calories they have consumed. Second, they are trying to atone or punish themselves for the food they have allowed themselves to eat. Just as self-harming behaviours are used to relieve anxiety, compensatory behaviours relieve the guilt or panic that people experience after eating.

Compensatory behaviours are often secretive so they can be hard to detect. Compensatory behaviours are very common in individuals as they begin their recovery: as they start to increase their calorie intake, they also increase their activity levels to deal with the guilt and fear they experience. With time, good nutrition, and weight restoration, the emotional reaction to eating should become less extreme. Talking therapies such as CBT can also help an individual understand why they feel compelled to 'compensate' for eating, and find other ways to deal with these distressing emotions.

COMPULSIVE EATING

See **BINGE-EATING DISORDER**.

COMPULSIVE EXERCISING

As we have seen, compensatory behaviour may take the form of frantic exercise after eating, to work off the calories consumed. Over-exercising is often undertaken compulsively or secretively, with individuals concealing the amount of exercise they are doing. They may be visiting a gym several times a day, increasing the duration and intensity of their exercise, especially after mealtimes. Exercise becomes a compulsion, and the individuals display distress when they are not able to exercise.

While physical activity is part of a healthy lifestyle, compulsive over-exercising is extremely unhealthy. Individuals will exercise through illness or injury or in freezing cold weather and will be unable to give themselves a rest day. When prevented from exercising, at home or in hospital, they are compelled to move constantly to burn off calories, walking around, up and down stairs, fidgeting or doing sit-ups or press-ups in secret.

CONSTIPATION

Chronic constipation is a common and distressing side effect of irregular eating. In anorexia, the diet may contain insufficient fibre or 'roughage' or simply insufficient calories overall. An anorexic individual's stomach may be receiving so little food that it cannot digest and move material through the waste system in the normal way. This causes delays in stomach emptying (see **GASTROPARESIS**) and reduced bowel activity. It can also cause the distressing sensation of 'fullness' – even when very little food has been eaten. In bulimia and binge-eating, excessive amounts of high-fat, high-sugar foods are difficult for the bowel to process. The gastrointestinal system is also disrupted by the constant stress of bingeing and purging.

In all cases, eating erratically and very large amounts or barely anything, the digestive system struggles to function normally. Reduced bowel functioning can lead to impairment or even total paralysis of the bowel, which may require surgery.

In addition, laxatives are a major cause of, and greatly exacerbate, constipation (see **LAXATIVES**).

CONTROL

Although a condition like anorexia revolves around rigid control and self-discipline, in fact the eating disorder itself is in control. Whatever your own personal rules, you are actually at the mercy of this cruel mental illness, unable to choose what, when and where you eat. Anorexia, bulimia and binge-eating rob you of control, making you unable to enjoy social occasions with others, limiting every area of your physical and mental health. The inability to enjoy eating also affects your family, friendships and romantic relationships.

Feeling guilty, panicky or out of control around food may have become second nature to you, but they are not normal or inevitable.

It's important to remember that you are not in control: the eating disorder is controlling you. Learning to challenge the rigid grip of your eating disorder is about taking back control, reclaiming your right to live and enjoy your life. (See also **EATING CONTROL**, **IMPROMPTU** and **WILLPOWER**.)

COPING STRATEGIES

Eating disorders are a reaction to stress, anxiety or emotional difficulties, but they do not work. Overeating or starving simply doesn't fix the problem – it doesn't fix any problem! (See **EMOTIONAL EATING**.) Instead, it's essential to find coping strategies that can actually help when times get tough.

We all go through difficult times in our lives. These range from minor stresses, such as delayed trains and traffic jams, to more serious problems, such as divorce, redundancy or bereavement. We cannot control what happens to us, but we can decide how we react. Many individuals with eating disorders take refuge in bingeing, purging or restricting food when they don't know how to cope with a situation. This illusion of *control* may temporarily alleviate the distressing sensation of feeling *out of control*, at the mercy of life's events.

In reality, harming oneself is never an effective coping strategy. Positive coping strategies are about finding genuine emotional support, and a way to cope with whatever life throws at us. Good examples might include confiding in a close friend or family member or finding a sympathetic therapist. Alternatively, it could be more practical: seeking financial advice for money worries, speaking to a colleague if it's a work problem, taking an online course or retraining if you need a change of direction. Joining support groups, talking to others and facing up to problems are always positive strategies – and always more effective than burying difficult emotions in food. (See also **JOURNAL**).

Note that although gentle physical exercise can be a beneficial coping strategy for many people, those with anorexia or orthorexia should *not* focus on exercise. If you are at risk of over-exercising, a hot bath is preferable to a workout.

COST

Eating disorders are mental illnesses with serious consequences. The physical, emotional, social and financial costs of severe eating disorders are incalculable. They take a toll on the person's health, on education and careers, on families and other close relationships. What starts as a straightforward diet, a desire to lose weight, may morph into something far more devastating.

In financial terms too, maintaining an eating disorder is expensive. Someone with bulimia or binge-eating may be consuming thousands of calories a day. That amount of food is expensive to purchase, and also difficult to hide.

Anorexia and orthorexia can be expensive too. Organic and so-called 'clean' foods carry a hefty premium. Special 'free-from' foods, gluten-free or dairy-free, cost several times more than their mainstream versions. There is a wider debate around the issue of unhealthy 'junk' food being cheaper, high in sugar and saturated fat, part of supermarkets' 2-for-1 offers – whereas healthier food, such as fresh fruit and vegetables, olive oil, nuts and organic ingredients almost always cost more.

CRAVINGS

Denying oneself certain foods or banning entire food groups invariably leads to greater cravings for that food. The 'forbidden fruit' comes to seem more desirable the more it's forbidden. This is why strict diets are rarely sustainable in the long term, and why it is unwise to demonize or label certain foods as 'bad' or unclean.

Cravings can be a particular problem for those with bulimia or BED, when repeated attempts to cut out *all* carbohydrates, for example, end in an uncontrollable binge. Paradoxically, being too controlled leads to a loss of control, and this causes the pernicious cycle of starving, bingeing and purging. In anorexia too, prolonged periods of restricted calorie intake make the individual more likely to binge, because at a certain point the hunger becomes extreme and unmanageable. This explains why many eating disorders swing between starving and bingeing, with periods of strict abstinence followed by overeating. The best way to avoid cravings is not to ban anything: if you enjoy chocolate or cake, say, have a small amount on a regular basis. Allowing yourself occasional treats is the most effective way to eliminate cravings.

CYCLOTHYMIA

This is a milder form of mood disturbance than bipolar disorder, but it has similar oscillations between elation and depression or highs and lows. Cyclothymic disorder is a combination of hypomania and dysthymic disorder, in which people experience 'high' periods of euphoria or mania, followed by 'low' periods of depression or despair. They display excessive physical and psychological energy during the highs, followed by sluggishness or lethargy during the lows. During the highs, they may move and talk rapidly, pacing about, exercising intensely and also jumping around intellectually, flitting from subject to subject, throwing themselves into new ventures with enthusiasm. Between the episodes of energy and elation, individuals have extreme low mood and feelings of hopelessness.

The cyclothymic swing between highs and lows could be days or even weeks depending on the individual, but it needs to have persisted for at least two years to be classified as cyclothymic disorder. While cyclothymia is less dangerous and distressing than bipolar disorder, it is certainly more than the simple daily fluctuations between good mood and occasional annoyance or bad temper experienced by most human beings. In the context of eating disorders, as with mood disorders in general, cyclothymic symptoms are exacerbated by erratic food intake, purging and bingeing, affecting emotional and hormonal balance, energy levels and sleep quality.

As yet, it is not clear whether cyclothymic disorder is a separate mental illness or a milder version of bipolar disorder.

DEHYDRATION

Dehydration occurs when more fluid is lost than is taken in, resulting in insufficient water for the body to function routinely. Chronic dehydration can cause circulatory disorders, electrolyte imbalance, seizures, permanent kidney damage, cardiac complications and even brain damage or death. The first signs of dehydration are extreme thirst, dry mouth and reduced urination; other symptoms include dry, itchy skin, sunken eyes, inability to produce tears, dizziness, weakness, darkening of the urine, fatigue and an elevated pulse rate. Swelling or puffiness in the fingers, ankles or face may indicate water retention (see **OEDEMA**), which has different causes from dehydration.

Dehydration in eating disorders is caused by fluid restriction, repeated vomiting, diuretic or laxative abuse and excessive exercise. Consuming insufficient calories also exacerbates dehydration, since a significant proportion of our daily fluid intake comes from food. (See also **ELECTROLYTE** and **KIDNEYS**.)

DEPRESSION

See **ANTIDEPRESSANTS** and **DEPRESSION**.

DEPRIVATION

At the heart of most disordered eating is a self-defeating cycle of deprivation and excess, famine and feast, all or nothing (see also **HUNGER** and **CRAVINGS**). It's human nature to want what we cannot have: this translates to high-sugar, high-fat or high-carb foods, often eaten in secret, in a rush, with a sense of guilt. When the body is deprived of regular, balanced nutrition our emotions and all our physiological functions get out of balance too, including hormone levels, body temperature, energy levels and cognitive abilities.

Clinicians consistently report the difficulty their anorexic patients have in responding to their own simple physiological needs. They describe the enforced discomfort that these individuals put themselves through, not eating when hungry, not sitting on soft chairs, not turning on the heating when cold. Most have no difficulty caring for others, nurturing friends (often feeding them obsessively) or caring for their children, but they are unable to do it for themselves. Self-deprivation is part of the illness.

DETOXING

The modern myth of detoxing says that we need expensive supplements or complicated fasting or juice cleansing regimes to detoxify ourselves. As with the clean eating movement, proponents of detoxifying refer liberally to 'toxins' and 'chemicals' – but remember, everything in our environment is a chemical, even water, H_2O! The truth is that normal food is not full of 'nasties', and our bodies do not require prolonged periods of fasting or strict raw food diets. Detoxification is a natural process, whereby the liver and other organs safely remove harmful or unwanted substances from the body. Anything the body does not need will be eliminated via the digestive system: no miracle potions, pills or patches will detox more effectively than a healthy liver!

Of course, there is nothing wrong with a period of healthy eating. You may wish to cut out alcohol after an indulgent Christmas, for example, or focus on increasing your intake of fresh fruit and vegetables. However, the notion of 'detoxing' is unhelpful and even triggering for those with restrictive eating disorders, particularly anorexia and orthorexia. It encourages a fearful faddy mindset in which 'normal' food is viewed as a threat. Restrictive detox cleanses can also trigger cravings for sugar, fat and other forbidden foods, which only worsens problems with binge-eating. Detox foods, teas and supplements are usually a waste of money, and extreme fasting (or detox) is unhealthy for those who are underweight. Instead, drink plenty of water and herbal teas, and eat as wide a variety of fresh, colourful foods as possible. (See also **CLEAN EATING** and **ORTHOREXIA**.)

DIARY/FOOD DIARY

See **JOURNAL**.

DIETING

Dieting is the single most important predictor of developing an eating disorder. In 2016, the American Academy of Pediatrics issued guidelines on preventing eating disorders and obesity. These suggested that parents should never talk about diets or weight (see also **FAMILY**). According to the report, 40 per cent of those admitted for eating disorders are dieters who have got out of control, tipping into anorexia or bulimia.

We live in a society obsessed with dieting, weight loss and getting the perfect body. Although it used to be a female concern, this weight obsession now affects men and even children too. Countless studies have found widespread body dissatisfaction among girls as young as six years old. Puberty and adolescence are especially dangerous times for undereating because the body is still growing. During this critical period, rapidly developing bodies already require at least 2,500 high-quality calories per day. Many teenage girls try to limit themselves to fewer than 1,000 calories a day. These are often junk food calories, lacking in the calcium, fats and other essential nutrients their growing bodies need.

Although eating disorders are far more complicated than just diets, they do begin as diets. While the majority of dieters will not become dangerously anorexic or bulimic, a significant proportion will. The prevalence of diets on every TV show, magazine or website sends out a clear message: thinner is better. Unsurprisingly, this inculcates the diet mindset among children, young people and adults, and may lead to a lifetime of always trying to lose weight, of restricting calories, vomiting after meals or binge-eating in secret. (See also **NORMAL DIET**.)

DIET PLAN

During recovery from an eating disorder, it can be helpful to follow a fixed diet plan. For those who are underweight, this will help ensure that they receive enough calories to begin gaining weight. In severe anorexia, it may include meal-replacement drinks or other calorie supplements. For those who are overweight or liable to overeat, a diet plan can help to minimize the impulse to binge. In all cases, making food choices in shops, cafés or restaurants is a stressful business: adhering to a structured plan takes the element of decision-making out of mealtimes.

The aim of a diet plan in recovery is to supply sufficient energy from carbohydrates, protein and fat to restore physical and mental health. A bulimia recovery plan will be very different from an anorexia recovery plan or a binge-eating recovery plan, but it will ensure that you meet all your nutritional and energy needs to underpin the other elements of recovery. It will also help to restore *regular* eating, which is essential for breaking out of the undereating or overeating cycle.

You will need to be strict with yourself if you are going to follow a meal plan: everything on the plan must be eaten, regardless of how you are feeling. At first it may seem intimidating or excessive or overly prescriptive, but remember that this is only a short-term aid. Meals and snacks should also be eaten at the same time every day, to retrain your body into a pattern of regular nutrition and digestion. Of course the long-term goal is to return to 'normal' eating like 'normal' people, not following specific rules or diet plans but simply responding to your body's natural hunger. However, in the short term, it can be reassuring to follow a structured meal plan. It can also provide useful guidance for the individual's family or partner living with them.

Your GP or therapist can refer you to a dietitian with specific expertise in eating disorders to help you draw up a plan, and this can be adjusted as your body begins to recover and your energy requirements change.

DISHONESTY

Eating disorders involve self-deception, secrecy, bargaining, legitimizing and flat-out lies. People lie to themselves and others all day long. They tell their parents or teachers they're not hungry or have already eaten. They steal or hide food, throw lunches in the bin, avoid meeting friends or lock themselves away to binge. They make deals with themselves about what they will and will not eat, what they deserve or how they should punish themselves.

In bulimia or binge-eating, this might take the form of indulgences or treats, such as, 'I haven't binged for three days so I deserve a blow-out tonight', or a more self-defeating tone, such as, 'Everyone ignored me at that party, which proves I'm fat and ugly, so I might as well go home and stuff my face.'

In anorexia, a similar process of legitimizing occurs. Individuals take any failure, however minor, as proof that they are not worthy of food. As they become more isolated, the fear of food and social interaction increases: 'I feel so alone, which proves I'm a loser, so I don't deserve to eat.'

In both undereating and overeating, minor setbacks can trigger extreme relapses. A bulimic who breaks his or her diet on a single occasion may plunge straight back into the cycle of bingeing and purging. An anorexic who ruins a family meal may take this as proof that he or she deserves to starve further, as punishment. Even positive behaviour, such as taking exercise or trying a new food, can trigger extreme behaviour. The person's inner monologue is full of self-defeating messages, often far harsher than they would use with a friend. This kind of irrational thinking is inevitable when the body and brain are starved of regular nutrition. Lies and deception are part of the confusion: you may no longer be able to recognize what's true and what's not, even in your own mind. The constant dishonesty is one of the most miserable parts of an eating disorder.

Don't despair. Eating regularly will help more than anything to clarify your thoughts and feelings. Make a start with three meals a day, however small. Find someone – a friend or counsellor – with whom you can be really honest. Tell them if you're engaging in risky behaviour or stealing money or food. Start a journal where you can write about what's really going on. Cut yourself some slack and try not to blame or punish yourself. The lies don't make you a bad person: rather, they are part of the illness. As you recover your health and break out of the cycle of starving, bingeing and purging, you will be able to be honest with yourself and those close to you.

DIURETICS

Diuresis is the process by which the kidneys flush out high levels of certain substances in the body, leading to an increased production of urine. Diuretics (or 'water pills') are medications that encourage the body to excrete additional water and sodium. They are prescribed for people with high blood pressure or heart failure, when the body holds too much water, for women who experience uncomfortable water retention during menstruation, and for certain kidney diseases. Most diuretics work by forcing the body to release more sodium into the urine; as the kidneys flush away excess sodium, they also flush away water. However, unnecessary use of diuretics interferes with normal kidney function and fluid levels. Increasing the volume of water and sodium excreted can lead to dangerous dehydration, oedema, weakness, nausea, abdominal pain and heart arrhythmia. Diuretics can also cause electrolyte imbalance, which can be potentially fatal.

Many individuals with eating disorders take diuretics, as they do laxatives, in the mistaken belief that they promote weight loss, when in fact they only promote water loss. Laxatives and diuretics do not lead to any loss of calories and are ineffective and unsafe for weight loss. Any apparent weight loss is due to a loss of body fluid and therefore temporary. The body protects against this loss of water by producing antidiuretic hormones (including aldosterone and renin), which are released in response to fluid loss. These hormones lead to water retention, which in turn leads to bloating and heaviness, and swelling around the eyes, stomach and ankles (see also **OEDEMA**).

If you have not been prescribed diuretics by your doctor, you do not need them. As with laxatives, the most important step in tackling diuretic abuse is to stop taking them. Gradually reducing the dose, while increasing good nutrition and drinking plenty of water, will help your kidneys and bladder return to normal.

Many herbs and natural substances are thought to have natural diuretic properties, including caffeine, green and black teas, citrus fruits and fruit juices, leafy green vegetables, onions, garlic, leeks, dandelion and ginger, so they will help your body to excrete any retained water in as natural a way as possible as your body adjusts. Cutting back on sodium, staying hydrated and being active will also help.

Low potassium levels are a dangerous side effect of diuretic misuse (see **ELECTROLYTES**). Symptoms include fatigue, thirst, palpitations or irregular heartbeat, muscle cramps or paralysis. If you experience any of these symptoms, you should seek medical advice immediately.

DRUGS

Sadly, no medication has yet been found that can cure eating disorders. These are complex conditions with both mental and physical roots; every person who has anorexia, bulimia, orthorexia, binge-eating or any related eating disorder will differ from every other person with these. However, some medication does help, specifically when it alleviates depression and reduces anxiety and obsessive compulsive behaviours.

Regular eating, that is breaking out of the cycle of starving, bingeing or purging, is clearly the most effective single tactic, but this is not available in pill form.

DRUNKOREXIA

Yet another one of the 'exias' that have been coined in recent years, drunkorexia involves 'saving' your calories for binge-drinking. The behaviour is disturbingly common among young women, when they starve themselves by day in order to drink large quantities of alcohol at night. Alcohol contains high levels of calories (in the form of sugar) but absolutely no nutritional benefits. All excessive drinking is unsafe, but large quantities of alcohol are even more dangerous when consumed on an empty stomach (see also **ALCOHOL**).

DSM

The *Diagnostic and Statistical Manual of Mental Disorders* is considered the universal authority for psychiatric diagnosis and classification of mental illnesses. Released by the highly influential American Psychiatric Association, the 5th edition came out in 2013. Crucially, this edition included significant changes to the classification of various eating disorders, such as the inclusion for the first time of BED as a recognized condition. For those involved in psychiatric illness, the DSM is the gold standard of mental health diagnosis.

EARLY INTERVENTION

One of the single most important aspects of the treatment of eating disorders is early intervention. It is clear that the sooner one intervenes to tackle disordered eating, the more effectively it can be treated. This is simply because disordered eating becomes habitual – and human beings are creatures of habit. The spiral of self-starving or binge-purging can be hard to escape. Early intervention is also essential from a health perspective: children and young adolescents who develop anorexia or bulimia may risk long-term physical damage at a time of crucial development (see **CHILDREN**), including delayed maturation and stunted growth. Socially, individuals with eating disorders also experience isolation and depression, which in turn affects their education, work and family lives. Physical, social and emotional problems tend to intensify over time, and the conditions become more difficult (and expensive) to treat. For all these reasons, spotting the warning signs, understanding the symptoms and intervening early are essential to the recovery process.

EATING CONTROL

As we have seen (see **CONTROL**), an eating disorder may look like being in control, but it's the exact opposite. In fact your entire life – your personal decisions, education, work, close relationships, mental and physical health – are at the mercy of a highly restrictive illness. Regaining control of your life starts with regaining control over your eating. This is not as hard as it sounds. The first step to getting your eating under control is to start eating regularly. Prolonged gaps between meals or continually restricting your food intake disrupts the body's healthy functioning, switching the metabolism into storage mode, which then risks weight gain as the balance between fat and lean tissue is disturbed. Eating late at night (see **NIGHT-EATING SYNDROME**) and other chaotic eating patterns also disrupt sleep, mood and hormones.

Regardless of whether you are underweight or overweight, the goal is to eat regular amounts of food throughout the day. In anorexia, this may be a schedule of three main meals as well as snacks, whereas in BED it may be smaller main meals: whatever form the disordered eating might take, regular meals are the best way to break out of the starve–binge–purge cycle.

Your daily intake should be spread fairly evenly across breakfast, lunch and dinner, with the majority of calories taken in before the evening. Aim for a balance of carbohydrates, protein and fat at every meal. Your carbohydrates might include bread, pasta, potatoes or rice; protein might include cheese, eggs, fish or beans; fat could include healthy oils, nuts and seeds and avocados. Eat hot food as well as cold, and solid food as well as liquid.

Take small amounts of regular exercise, such as a gentle stroll, but not immediately after eating and not excessively. This helps to balance emotions and keep the metabolism ticking over.

Other helpful tips for regaining control include staying calm around food: disordered eating results in panic and guilt around the simple act of eating, so try to avoid this. Eat at a table in the kitchen or dining room. Make each meal an enjoyable occasion; set yourself a place using proper plates, cutlery and a napkin. Bring your plate in from another room, away from food containers and cupboards, and sit down to eat. Don't distract yourself with TV, radio or reading. Look at the food on your plate, breathe and swallow between bites, take time to enjoy the smell and taste of your meal.

Eat with family or friends if possible. Eating with others is very helpful during the recovery phase: not only does it renormalize the act of eating socially but it also helps to avoid the risk of chaotic patterns such as bingeing or overeating or using excessive salt, spices or sweeteners. Crucially, eating with others also reminds you what normal portion sizes look like.

Reintroducing regular eating can be hard at first, but stick with it. Don't panic if you feel full (in anorexia) or still hungry (in bulimia or binge-eating). Stay at the table, perhaps with a piece of fruit or a herbal tea, chatting with others. This allows time for nutrients to be absorbed into the bloodstream, so that your hunger feels satisfied and digestion can begin. It should also – hopefully – make eating a less anxious experience!

Once you have managed to regularize your daily meals, it's time to experiment: see **IMPROMPTU**.

EATING DISORDER NOT OTHERWISE SPECIFIED (ED-NOS)

This is a surprisingly common diagnosis. ED-NOS describes cases where a person may not fit the precise pattern of eating disorders such as anorexia but still experiences significant distress due to an unhealthy psychological relationship with food. This diagnosis recognizes that many individuals display a range of disordered behaviours around food. It is rare for someone to be purely anorexic, for example, or purely bulimic: restrictive eating will often tip over into bingeing and purging. Individuals may relapse into disordered behaviours at times of intense stress as a coping mechanism. Someone who overeats may vomit only occasionally; someone who restricts their food may sometimes binge too. Labels such as **BULIMAREXIA** also reflect these mixed disordered conditions. (See also **ORTHOREXIA**.)

ELDERLY

Eating disorders do not only affect the young. In fact, anorexia is becoming increasingly common among elderly women. There are two reasons for this increase. First, eating disorders have become more common over the past three or four decades, and therefore many women are living their whole lives (and reaching old age) with unresolved problems. Second, even older women may be feeling the ever-increasing social pressures to be slim. In our youth-and-beauty-obsessed society, elderly women may pursue thinness as a way of coping with the ageing process. Adopting a healthy lifestyle is important in middle and later age to avoid a wide range of ageing risks, including osteoporosis, dementia, stroke and heart disease – but remember, obsessive weight loss and compulsive exercising can affect anyone at any age.

The diagnostic criteria for anorexia in the elderly are similar to those for younger people, including self-induced starvation, fear of fatness, avoidance of eating situations and denial of the problem. However, the causes of eating disorders in the elderly are complex: a woman may have been preoccupied all her life with weight and dieting or it may be linked to ageing, loneliness, physical or psycho-logical changes. Sudden weight loss may begin as a medical problem, after an operation or illness, for example, but then morph into an inability to regain a healthy weight. Eating disorders can be hard to detect among the elderly who live alone, who may not have anyone looking out for them. Elderly women have already gone through the menopause, so amenorrhoea is not relevant as a diagnostic criterion. Older women may also be less likely to discuss emotional problems with doctors, psychiatrists or even friends – they may feel ashamed of struggling with a 'young person's problem' or simply be reluctant to open up.

It should be remembered that the elderly are just as vulnerable to social and emotional life stressors as younger people, as well as having to deal with the loneliness and bereavement that often come in later life. Older women (and men) are at risk of developing eating disorders as a way of coping with these specific challenges. (See also **LATE ONSET**.)

ELECTROLYTES

These are salts in the body that are essential for metabolic processes. Electrolytes contribute to the healthy functioning of muscle and nerve cells, as well as the body's main organs, including the brain, heart and kidneys. Electrolytes carry electrical charges when dissolved in solution. They are vital for maintaining the body's complex physical balance.

Individuals with eating disorders frequently have fluid or electrolyte abnormalities, due to vomiting, laxative or diuretic abuse, low salt intake or dehydration. Electrolyte disturbance is in fact one of the most dangerous complications of bulimia nervosa: repeated vomiting can seriously deplete the essential electrolytes potassium, chloride and sodium.

Electrolyte imbalance can cause weakness, exhaustion, constipation and depression. People may experience muscle cramps, tingling or pins and needles, due to the imbalance of these essential salts. In the most serious cases, electrolyte imbalance can result in cardiac arrest and sudden death.

EMETICS

These are substances that induce vomiting. Some individuals with bulimia are unable to make themselves sick after eating or want to vomit more, so they take emetics. Excessive and inappropriate use of these medicines can seriously damage the heart.

EMOTIONAL EATING

'Emotional eating' is using food for reasons other than hunger and fuel. It's using food to suppress pain or cheer ourselves up, to mitigate boredom or avoid facing our demons. Mindless eating occurs when we're hardly aware of what we're consuming. Many individuals who experience emotional eating are a normal weight. It only becomes problematic when food becomes a way of avoiding important emotions; when you feel upset or angry or ashamed and you turn to food instead.

The majority of eating disorders are emotional, not physical, in nature. Individuals with anorexia or bulimia did not start out with a fundamental food problem: rather, they are struggling with difficult emotions, thoughts or beliefs. In the absence of coping strategies, these emotional problems have been translated into disordered eating behaviour. Others may subsume their problems into different habits, drugs or alcohol, for example, but for these people, it's food. Maybe starving or bingeing helped them to suppress or avoid their emotions once, but it does not solve anything in the long term. Once the disordered eating behaviour itself becomes habitual, it also becomes a physical problem, which fuels loneliness, social isolation and low self-esteem.

It is hard to separate emotional eating from normal eating because eating is inherently emotional in nature. Food is intimately linked with our emotions: hunger affects our mood. From our earliest mother's milk, food represents caring and nurture. We cook for friends to express our love, we come together for family meals, birthday dinners, picnics. All over the world, different cultures celebrate their important occasions by eating together. When we are far from home, familiar food is very comforting.

Eating to celebrate or soothe is normal, but it can go too far, such as when we come to rely on food to suppress or numb our feelings. And emotional eating is not just overeating: emotional not-eating or starving is equally problematic. In other words, emotional eating affects those who are emaciated and those who are obese. It's usually at the root of restrictive anorexia just as much as it is at the root of BED. Physically, these individuals look very different from each other: one is very underweight, one is very overweight. It is therefore assumed that they have very different problems. However, inside they are not so different after all. Food is used as a defence mechanism, a way of hiding, a way of numbing or suppressing emotions that feel unmanageable. Fatness can be a way of hiding from the world (and from the problems of physical attractiveness), just as extreme thinness can. Both experiences can feel like disappearing.

EMOTIONS

There is a wonderful saying: 'You should feel your feelings and eat your food'. So often, though, we get them mixed up. (See also **EMOTIONAL EATING**.)

EXERCISE

In general, taking regular physical exercise is positive. The UK's Department of Health guidelines recommend that adults take at least 150 minutes of moderate aerobic activity, such as cycling or fast walking, or 75 minutes of vigorous activity, such as running, every week. The benefits are clear: exercise is good for our cardiovascular and respiratory systems, for physical fitness, strength and flexibility, and for overall mental well-being. However, studies have found that up to 80 per cent of UK adults do not take enough exercise.

At the other end of the spectrum, some are taking far too much. For individuals with anorexia or orthorexia, excessive exercise can exert a dangerous toll on an already malnourished or weakened body. It is often assumed that the less you eat, the less exercise you can do, but sadly many people persevere with strenuous physical exertion to the point of near-collapse.

Remember the equation: calories in versus calories out. It stands to reason that the more exercise you do, the more you should eat. In anorexia (and orthorexia), although the duration and intensity of exercise increase, calorie intake does not. Excessive exercise makes the person lose yet more weight, and places the weakened heart under stress. It risks damaging fragile bones – broken bones and fractures are common in individuals with anorexia (see also **OSTEOPOROSIS/OSTEOPENIA**). It also causes muscle wasting: when there is no fat to burn as fuel, the body begins to eat away at its own muscle. All these problems are exacerbated by an insufficient intake of protein, to rebuild muscles, and calcium, for healthy bones. With severe anorexia, individuals who work out furiously cannot build strength because their muscles are atrophying. Even strong, healthy young men have collapsed under strenuous training conditions – so, for those with severe eating disorders, so-called high-intensity interval training is potentially very dangerous. Exercise can also be dangerous in those with bulimia who are at risk of cardiac irregularities and electrolyte imbalance.

Taking a lot of exercise (see also **ADDICTION**) is an understandable response to anorexia and orthorexia: in a depressed, semi-starved brain, levels of the mood regulator serotonin are very low. The rush of endorphins known as the 'runner's high' actually provides a temporary boost to a depressed, starving brain.

Athletes often show signs of exercise addiction, combining intense physical exertion with calorie restriction. Eating disorders are particularly common in sports dependent on weight control, and sports where the body is minimally clad and highly scrutinized, such as in female gymnasts or ballerinas. Unhealthy exercise and eating behaviours are also found to affect male athletes in sports where weight control matters, such as jockeys and boxers. Before a race or a big fight, for example, many jockeys and lighter-weight boxers deprive themselves of food and even fluids to 'make the weight'. (See also **ATHLETIC TRIAD**.)

Anyone with an eating disorder should consider low-impact forms of exercise, such as yoga or gentle pilates. Stretching, deep breathing and relaxation exercises are also therapeutic.

EXTREMES

Whether it's extreme calorie restriction, bingeing or purging, or simply trying every new dietary fad going, individuals with eating disorders tend to go to extremes. It is not clear whether they are predisposed to extreme behaviour or their condition causes it, but it is likely a combination of the two. Other impulsive or disinhibited behaviours, for example drinking, gambling or risky sexual encounters, are also seen in those with bulimia or BED.

FAILURE

Failing does not make you a failure. This is a useful mantra, especially for those with eating disorders (see **COGNITIVE IMPAIRMENT**). Whether it's failing to try a new food (in anorexia) or overeating (in bulimia), a single failure is just that. Failing once or several times does not mean you won't ever overcome your problems. In fact, in studies of people giving up smoking, the best predictor of success was how many times the person had tried to give up. The more times they tried, the more likely they were to succeed in the end.

Each time you challenge the eating-disordered behaviour, the anorexic voice in your head or the overwhelming urge to binge, it will make you stronger. You're not failing, you're learning and prac-tising and preparing to beat this problem. Take something positive from each attempt: when you fail, fail forward. Write down your feelings (see **COPING STRATEGIES** and **JOURNAL**) and work out what you could do differently next time. There are plenty of self-help books, business gurus and inspiring real-life stories and blogs out there, and they really can help. Find your favourite mantras, write them on sticky notes and put them up around your home or just repeat them when you need to stay on track.

FAMILY

Family members have a crucial but difficult role in the context of eating disorders. Parents and siblings can be a much-needed source of support, especially during recovery. However, serious eating dis-orders cause tension and conflict within families: like many other mental illnesses, they affect everyone, not just the individual.

It is important to remember that no one is to 'blame' for an eating disorder. In many cases, particularly anorexia nervosa, mothers feel responsible for their child's illness: did they inadvertently feed them the wrong food or criticize their appearance or set a bad example? Interesting research is being carried out on the heritability of anorexia and genetics, but there is no conclusive evidence as yet. Eating disorders are likely to be a combination of genetics *and* environment, nature *and* nurture. Parents should not blame themselves.

Mealtimes are an integral part of family life, and are often the only time when everyone gets to sit down together and talk about their day. Disordered eating disrupts this family time, and mealtimes can become a battleground with anxious parents watching – and pretending not to watch – every bite their eating-disordered child takes. Non-affected siblings may understandably feel resentful at the extra attention their ill sibling receives, and angry or confused at the situation.

Despite the difficulties, families can play a beneficial role in preventing eating disorders in the first place. Parents are most likely to pick up on early signs of disordered eating, and therefore have a crucial role to play in preventing anorexia or bulimia from becoming more severe. Early behavioural signs of anorexia include secrecy or furtiveness around food, avoiding family meals and social meals, always claiming 'I've already eaten', cutting out 'bad' foods and becoming irritable, withdrawn or preoccupied. Similar signs may appear in bulimia, as may disappearing to the bathroom straight after meals, stashing food or hiding empty food packaging, and using laxatives. Compulsive exercise, constant dieting and excessive concern over body shape and weight are, of course, common in all eating disorders.

The advice for parents is clear: don't talk about dieting with your child – emphasize healthy eating and physical activity instead. Encourage them to feel positive about their bodies (half of teenage girls and a quarter of boys say they dislike their shape). Try to avoid gossiping about other women's bodies in front of your children or obsessing over your own diet. And eat together as much as possible:

studies consistently find that regular family dinners reduce the occurrence of eating disorders. Try to keep the channels of communication open – talk about concerns you may have. And when necessary, seek professional help as early as possible.

FAT

Fat is essential for the human body. Every one of our organs, from skin to brain, eyes to joints to reproductive systems, requires essential fats for optimal functioning. Essential fats reduce the risk of heart disease, cancer, arthritis, allergies, eczema, depression, infection, fatigue, infertility – and much more.

Individuals with anorexia nervosa avoid all energy-dense foods, but most particularly fat. For obvious reasons, healthy dietary fats are associated with *being* fat: as if any fat that is consumed will immediately appear on the body as fat. Since fat is the most energy-dense food, many diets are based on restricting fat intake, and fat has been demonized for decades. The greatest fear in anorexia, that of gaining weight and getting fat, is therefore linked to eating essential fats, and the person cuts out this rich, life-giving nutrient.

Fat deficiency has serious consequences. Physically, a body starved of fat begins to waste: in the absence of adequate fat stores, energy is taken instead from muscles, so muscles start to atrophy. Without fat, reproductive capacity is reduced, brain power is depleted, skin becomes dry and flaky, and hair and nails become brittle and weak. Fat is also a carrier of water, and every cell in the human body depends on this to stay plump and hydrated.

Essential fats fuel the body and stimulate the metabolism. Cutting out fat prevents the body from absorbing many other dietary nutrients, which is why we need a balance of fat, protein and carbohydrates at every meal. Fat gives flavour to food and satiates, whereas low-fat foods tend to leave people hungry and wanting more. For example, in low-fat yogurts the intrinsic flavour is concentrated in the fat element. The more fat is skimmed off, the less flavour the yogurt has, which is why low-fat versions tend to contain artificial sweeteners and flavourings, to make up for the lack of taste, as well as thickeners to improve consistency. In recent decades, low-fat regimes that reinforced the (inaccurate) link between eating fat and getting fat sent generations of dieters into unhealthy patterns of eating.

Like following a low-carb diet (see **CARBOHYDRATES**), following a low-fat diet affects your concentration and mood. It makes you more likely to crave the 'forbidden' substance, and hence more likely to binge. And low-fat diets don't work. All the evidence shows that Mediterranean-style diets plentiful in essential fats lead to slimmer, healthier, longer-lived populations with a lower risk of cardiovascular disease.

While demonizing fat may be unwise, it is clear that there are such things as 'good' and 'bad' fats. We cannot ignore the increase in obesity and obesity-related illnesses. Most people in the West consume too much saturated (or bad) fats, such as meat, spreads and high-fat processed or 'fast' food, and too few essential (or good) fats. It's clear that we could all benefit from more essential fats in our diets: good sources include oils such as hemp, linseed/flax and pumpkin oils, seeds, nuts, oily fish and avocados.

FEAR

As we have seen, emotions play a central role in eating disorders. Depression, loneliness and anxiety are often cited, but fear also plays a significant role. People with anorexia fear above all losing control: they maintain strict dietary rules for fear of what might happen if they allowed themselves to eat. Those with BED may fear what would happen if they lost a lot of weight and others found them attractive.

Many of these fears are 'What if . . .?' fears: What if I managed to get back to eating normally with others? What if I listened to my appetite, and trusted my body? What if I allowed myself to eat enough, not too little and not too much? (see **HUNGER**). What if I managed to get back to a healthy, happy weight – what would I be expected to do in the world, and what if I failed?

Many individuals with anorexia react badly to change: different foods, different routines of any sort, fill them with fear. Being ill or different, maintaining the condition, is a sort of safety net.

One of the most frightening aspects of eating disorders is, paradoxically, a fear of recovery. Over time, disordered eating habits become reassuring. These may be secretive routines around eating or exercise, stocking up on 'special' foods or planning a binge in private. Shopping and hoarding and purging in secret give a structure to the person's daily life. However distressing and self-limiting these habits are to maintain, they can be very hard to kick. For many people, the eating disorder is part of their identity: 'If I'm not anorexic, who will I be?' For all the misery and illness, the eating disorder may even be a friend. If there have been medical complications, requiring hospital stays or regular group therapy, the loss of these appointments may fill the person with fear. If they have missed out on school, college or getting a job, the future without their eating disorder may appear frightening and empty.

It is important to understand that 'fear' to someone with a severe eating disorder isn't like everyday nerves or worry. The fear of fat, for example, seen in anorexia, is closer to a phobia. Faced with eating high-calorie or fattening foods, individuals will be paralysed. It becomes almost impossible for an anorexic person to eat voluntarily, hence the need for constant reassurance and support. Similarly, someone with severe bulimia may experience extreme panic when he or she cannot vomit after eating or is denied access to laxatives. These fears are not impossible to treat, and they will decrease over time – but they should not be underestimated.

Fear of recovery does not make sense to healthy outsiders, but it's very real to the person. Supporting them through recovery step by step, helping them to find a real reason to recover, is therefore essential. (See also **EARLY INTERVENTION** and **MOTIVATION**.)

FERTILITY AND INFERTILITY

One of the main physical indicators of anorexia in women is amenorrhoea, or absence of periods, which affects female fertility. In cases of low body weight and inadequate nutrition, the ovaries temporarily shut down and menses cease. When calories are very low, reproduction is not a priority – in fact, conception may actually be a risk. Prolonged amenorrhoea has damaging effects on bone density (see **OSTEOPOROSIS/OSTEOPENIA**) and is a key warning sign that body weight is unhealthily low. Low body weight can also affect sperm quality, and hence male fertility.

The good news is that fertility almost always recovers with restoration of weight and nutrition. When weight and body fat return to healthy levels, hormone levels return to normal, stimulating ovulation and regular periods.

FRIENDS

Like family, friends hold an important but sometimes uncomfortable role within the context of eating disorders. Schoolfriends or workmates are often the first to pick up on problem behaviour, such as noticing if someone is skipping meals or going to the bathroom straight after eating. However, they may also feel powerless to do anything or disloyal if they report their concerns to a teacher or parent. Equally, though, friends may be in a good position to discuss the problem, as they are closer in age and attitude.

In severe eating disorders, such as hospitalization for anorexia, the person often feels very alone. Not only are they missing out on valuable school or work time, but they are also missing out on the fun of being with friends. The person will also be avoiding meals with friends, pub lunches – and any social situation involving food. It is important for both the person and their friends to make an effort to maintain friendships despite the eating difficulties: close friends can be a valuable source of support during illness and recovery.

g

GASTROINTESTINAL COMPLICATIONS

Disordered eating causes significant digestive and gastric problems. Instead of food being consumed at a normal rate, at normal intervals, via the normal process of chewing, swallowing and absorption, the individual may consume large amounts rapidly, vomit repeatedly or starve themselves of nutrition altogether. This seriously disrupts normal digestive functioning, as the oesophagus, stomach, intestines and bowel struggle to cope with erratic eating patterns.

A common problem for bulimic individuals is delayed stomach emptying (see **GASTROPARESIS**). Food remains in the stomach for longer than usual due to repeated bingeing, purging and fasting, which disrupts the body's normal gastric process. Self-induced vomiting can seriously damage the oesophagus and stomach. The digestive process slows down, making the individual feel uncomfortably bloated. Anorexics may feel very full after consuming only a small amount of food. Using laxatives or emetics to tackle the problem only disrupts the gastric process further. Once normal eating is restored, the stomach, bowel and digestive processes should return to normal. However, the sooner this happens, the better, because damage can be permanent.

GASTROPARESIS

This term describes slowed emptying of the stomach. The gastrointestinal system responds to calorie restriction and weight loss by slowing down. This causes bloating, a sensation of fullness, nausea, acid reflux and even vomiting – all of which may reinforce disordered eating habits. It is essential not to restrict the diet further or misdiagnose these symptoms as intolerances (see **INTOLERANCE/ALLERGY**). Increasing fibre and fluid intake will help, but the only way to resolve the problem is restoration to a healthy weight and regular nutrition.

GLUTEN

Gluten is a protein found in grains like wheat, rye and barley, and commonly present in widely consumed foods such as bread and pasta. In recent years, gluten has been singled out as the cause of many perceived digestive problems (see **INTOLERANCE/ ALLERGY**). Gluten has also become a target of the clean eating movement (see **CLEAN EATING** and **ORTHOREXIA**). It is estimated that around 8.5 million people a year in the UK consume gluten-free products. What was once a niche eating habit has become mainstream.

For a small proportion of the global population – around 1 per cent – avoiding gluten is essential. These people have coeliac disease, and their immune system mistakes gluten for a threat and attacks it, damaging the intestine in the process. Another tiny proportion, around 0.01 per cent may have a genuine wheat allergy. However, these are medically recognized conditions and can be diagnosed with straightforward tests.

Around 15 per cent of the population believe that going gluten-free is healthy or they have found that it relieves symptoms such as bloating or wind. In fact, these are common digestive complaints, and testing rarely reveals any allergies or gut inflammation. The vast majority of those who believe themselves to be gluten or wheat intolerant are not.

Clearly, avoiding gluten is a personal choice. However, in the context of disordered eating, especially anorexia nervosa, it can further limit an already highly restrictive diet. Cutting out gluten becomes yet another rule and a way of avoiding 'normal' foods. It can also lead to serious nutritional deficiencies: many regular products containing gluten also contain carbohydrates, which are an important source of energy.

Many common digestive symptoms are more likely to be the result of disordered eating. Those with anorexia who are eating very little may experience discomfort or constipation, while those who are bingeing and purging may experience bloating or stomach pain. This is the digestive system under stress, without regularity, and either too empty or too full, disrupted by laxatives and vomiting. With the gradual restoration of regular meals and balanced nutrition, these digestive symptoms should resolve without the need to ban gluten from your diet.

GUILT

Like fear and shame, guilt is an experience common to almost all individuals with an eating disorder. In anorexia, there is guilt at voluntarily eating anything, no matter how small; in bulimia, guilt after purging and a feeling of self-disgust; in binge-eating, guilt at overeating, at being overweight or greedy. It is paradoxical that such different conditions should have these intense emotions in common, but in fact someone with anorexia may feel just as greedy and ashamed as a larger person does. Both may avoid eating in public, for fear of being looked at, as if the act of eating itself were somehow shameful. One of the best ways to combat this nagging sense of guilt and greed is to understand why our bodies need food and how it fuels every biological process that takes place. Indeed, in recovery many people become near-experts in nutrition! This learning process helps to assuage the emotional aspect of the illness: eating is not greedy, it's essential to human life.

Paradoxically, looking at others may also help with guilt. This does not mean comparing your own weight or body shape to that of celebrities or supermodels, but simply observing the world around you. Look at your siblings, colleagues or friends (see also **ROLE MODELS**). Look at ordinary people going about their daily lives, grabbing a sandwich in a café or shopping in the supermarket. They are healthy, happy and active. They eat a normal amount of food, they eat in public, they eat at regular intervals during the day – and then they get on with their lives. Compared with the guilt, secrecy and shame of an eating disorder, this 'normal' eating looks liberating. Try it for a day and see how you get on.

HAIR

Just like skin, nails and teeth, our hair is an outer sign of our inner health. The cells in every strand of hair need to be nourished with essential fats, protein and a variety of vitamins and minerals. Our so-called 'crowning glory' suffers greatly from crash dieting and poor nutrition: in those who are starving, hair becomes dry and brittle, and the scalp becomes flaky.

As hair is made of protein, this is one of the most important sources for making hair strong and healthy. Extremely low-protein diets may result in hair loss and thinning. Chicken, turkey, fish, dairy products and eggs are excellent sources of protein, along with vegetarian sources such as yogurt, cheese, legumes and nuts. Iron is also crucial for providing the roots and follicles of our hair with a rich blood supply. Vitamins A, C and E, omega-3 fatty acids, zinc and selenium are also essential for strong, shiny hair. Biotin is a water-soluble B vitamin found in foods such as wholegrains, liver, egg yolk, soya flour and yeast.

The good news is that hair grows quickly, and therefore responds rapidly to improved nutrition.

HEART

See **CARDIAC COMPLICATIONS**.

HOARDING

A compulsion that stems from the belief certain objects cannot be discarded because they might be needed later. While the term 'hoarding' is used casually in everyday life, in recent years hoarding has also been identified as a form of OCD. For many individuals, hoarding behaviour is strongly associated with their disordered eating. It is usually food hoarding, but also extends to general hoarding (see also **KLEPTOMANIA**). The correlation between disordered eating and hoarding tendencies is not entirely understood, but we know that serotonin dysfunction has been implicated in OCD as well as in anorexia and bulimia nervosa. Hoarding has often been noted in those with eating disorders and vice versa. The two disorders share key traits, including indecisiveness, anxiety, depression, social dysfunction and possibly genetic links.

HUNGER

Perhaps the most important aspect of recovering from an eating disorder is learning (or relearning) to listen and respond to your hunger. From birth, our body's hunger signals are primal and elemental: they are essential to human survival. The problem comes when we mess with these hunger signals. As soon as we start dieting, start bingeing, fast intermittently, avoid certain foods or whole food groups, our body becomes confused. Chaotic overeating or restrictive undereating interferes with the natural cycle of hunger and satiety. As we have already seen (in **DEPRIVATION** and **CRAVINGS**), the more we deprive ourselves, the more we crave unhealthy foods. Similarly, the hungrier our body and brain become, the less able we are to make rational choices. By dieting or fasting, we risk losing control and bingeing on unhealthy 'fast' food, rather than making nutritious, balanced choices.

The notion that anorexic individuals are simply not hungry or have lost their appetite is incorrect (see also **APPETITE**). They are on the edge of starvation all the time, but they are very frightened of responding to that hunger. They fear that if they respond to their hunger by eating, they will never be able to stop. Many people with anorexia deny experiencing hunger at all. Eventually, they may reach the point of being uncertain about what spontaneous hunger actually feels like.

Bulimia and binge-eating also interfere with the body's natural hunger signals. People who consume very large quantities of food at a single sitting are not – strictly speaking – hungry at all. They cram the food down quickly, barely registering or tasting it, experiencing physical discomfort and self-loathing afterwards. Because they are not registering the feeling of fullness, they may continue to the point of feeling (or being) physically sick. This disconnect means that when they are hungry, they may feel that bingeing and/or vomiting are their only options.

In both overeating and undereating, the natural response to hunger has gone haywire. Learning what hunger feels like – sitting with a sensation of hunger, maybe sipping some water first – can be a revelation. Rate your hunger from 1 to 10, waiting until it's a 5 or 6. Then, before you start eating, focus carefully on what your taste-buds and stomach are actually hungry for. Something light or more substantial? Something hot or cold? Something savoury or sweet?

If you're finding it hard to distinguish between physical hunger and other emotions – such as boredom, sadness or anger – you could record these feelings in a food diary (see **COPING STRAT-EGIES** and **JOURNAL**). Instead of reaching for the same old snacks, try preparing yourself some nutritious meals with interesting ingredients. Plan ahead before you go shopping: this can help avoid a binge episode. Make a list of what you need to buy and don't go to the supermarket when you're ravenous. (See **DIET PLAN** for how to draw up a structured daily eating schedule.)

Hunger is about trust: trusting our body to tell us when we're hungry, what we're hungry for and when to stop.

HYPOMANIA

See **CYCLOTHYMIA**.

HYPOTHALAMUS

A small gland located centrally and towards the base of the brain, the hypothalamus is involved in satiation or the feeling of fullness.

The hypothalamus regulates appetite in an area of the brain where hormones and other chemicals that control hunger and appetite are made. The hypothalamus controls the release of neuropeptide Y and peptide YY in the gut; in normal eating patterns, these two chemicals work together to indicate fullness after a meal.

Other chemicals are also involved in hunger signals, notably the hormone leptin, which has been shown to be produced by fat cells. Leptin appears to tell your body how much fat is stored, thus regulating hunger, and also reduces the hypothalamus's secretion of neuropeptide Y.

Prolonged disordered eating can result in serious disruption of the body's hormonal signals: by not responding to severe hunger signals (in anorexia) or by ignoring signals of satiation (in bulimia or binge-eating) the individual loses touch with his or her own natural cues.

Amenorrhoea –the cessation of menstrual periods – may be due to dysfunction of the hypothalamus (as well as loss of body fat). As in hypothermia, which also results from disruptions in the action of the hypothalamus, these endocrine abnormalities affect many different body functions (see **HYPOTHERMIA**).

HYPOTHERMIA

Reduced body temperature is extremely common in individuals with low weight. The brain's hypothalamus maintains the body's base temperature, and this is one of the core endocrine functions that becomes disrupted in anorexia. The body's base temperature is reduced, and individuals struggle to adjust to temperature changes. Additionally, they are eating very little fuel – calories generate heat – and are also extremely thin. Humans need their subcutaneous fat to stay warm; an emaciated person does not have this insulation. Being constantly cold (even in summer), wearing several layers of clothing and huddling up to radiators are characteristic anorexic behaviours. The growth of downy body hair (see **LANUGO**) is another way the body attempts to conserve heat.

i

IMMUNE SYSTEM

The immune system is responsible for defending the body when it is attacked by disease. It's a complex system of cells, tissues and organs that protect us from invasive or infectious organisms. Poor nutrition, crash dieting and repeated vomiting all put the body under stress. Without a regular supply of nutrients the immune system is weakened and unable to fight off infections.

IMPROMPTU

The first priority in disordered eating is to re-establish regular daily food habits. As we have seen (in **EATING CONTROL**), making time for three meals a day – and snacks too if you are underweight – will not only help you maintain a healthy weight but also balance your mood and improve your sleep. Irregular eating increases the risk of extreme hunger, losing control and chaotic bingeing.

Now that you are back in control, paradoxically it's time to practise letting go! Impromptu or *unplanned* eating is important in everyday life – but incredibly difficult for those with eating disorders. You may have drawn up your own food schedule or agreed it with your dietitian or therapist, and it is important to keep following this. At first, this may be a narrow, repetitive range of foods, carefully balanced for health reasons, and foods that you feel 'safe' with. However, as you recover, you should also try to branch out. At the heart of eating disorders is anxiety and fear around food. The goal, ultimately, is to get back to a healthy, happy attitude to food. (See also **ROLE MODELS**.)

Impromptu eating can mean almost anything – but it should challenge you. For example, try accepting a friend's invitation to cook dinner, going to a restaurant where you haven't checked the menu or simply buying a different sandwich without scrutinizing the label.

Experiment with your other routines too, not just with food. Practise spontaneity. Take a new route to work, wear a new colour, listen to a new radio station. When you get used to trying new experiences, other changes will feel less threatening. Remember, an eating disorder limits your whole world, not just the food you eat: being adventurous will expose you to new people, places, flavours and feelings. When you challenge your fears – 'If I eat that food I'll gain weight', 'If I start eating I'll never be able to stop', 'If I eat in public people will stare at me' – you will usually prove yourself wrong. Eat something unplanned and do something impromptu every day.

INFERTILITY

See **FERTILITY** and **INFERTILITY**.

INJURY

As we saw earlier (in **EXERCISE**), undereating and starving put a dangerous strain on the individual. Without adequate protein for healthy muscles and calcium for healthy bones, the body is permanently weakened. Injury is therefore common, from simple overexertion, strains and sprains to actual broken bones (see **OSTEOPOROSIS/OSTEOPENIA**). Injury is almost inevitable with insufficient calories and insufficient rest. When the body runs out of its preferred fuel – fat – it breaks down muscle instead, causing weak muscles, joints and bones. It can also damage vital organs such as the heart. Cardiac arrest is a real risk for individuals with eating disorders, particularly anorexia, orthorexia and bulimia. Palpitations, dizziness and chest pains are signs that you should stop exercising immediately and seek medical help.

Fuelling your body before and after exercise is crucial: running on empty will cause injuries and may even have fatal consequences.

INSOMNIA

See **SLEEP HYGIENE**.

INSULA

Over the past decade, research into an area of the brain known as the insula has led to new insights into the causes and treatment of drug and alcohol addictions, anxiety and eating disorders.

The insula is a small structure, around the size of a prune, located deep in the cerebral cortex. In brain scans, the insula lights up when we experience complicated human emotions, such as pain, empathy, lust and disgust. The insula receives different physiological messages from all over the body and translates them into feelings, decisions and actions. It is connected to multiple neurological networks and also works as a communication hub or bridge between the right and left sides of the brain. The insula has been called the 'wellspring of social emotions', a unique area of the brain that provides insight into what it means to be human.

The insula is particularly interesting in the context of eating disorders. It monitors a wide range of functions, including controlling anxiety, regulating feelings of disgust, communicating hunger and perceptions of taste, processing sensations of pain and maintaining an accurate experience of body image. In studies of anorexic individuals, scientists have found abnormal blood flow to the insula, indicating that the insula is not functioning properly. This explains familiar characteristics of anorexia such as distorted body image and altered perception, as well as the ability to block signals of hunger and pain. It may also explain the rigid cognitive thinking – the inability to see the wood for the trees – that is familiar to anyone with anorexia.

The insula also monitors satiety and bodily awareness. When there is too much of the stress hormone norepinephrine in the insula, as there often is in the brains of anorexic individuals, these senses are distorted: some anorexics feel full when their stomachs are empty, some see a 'fat' person when they look in the mirror. Their pain threshold is often elevated, enabling them to withstand the most extreme hunger pangs, for example. Their fight-or-flight response is permanently switched on. People with anorexia exist in a state of hyperarousal or panic, and these emotions seem to attach themselves to food. Eating situations are perceived as threatening, not pleasurable, to be avoided at all costs.

The understanding of the brain's role in severe eating disorders is still at an early stage, but the insula is now of great interest to neuro-scientists within the field.

INSULIN

The hormone insulin is produced by the pancreas and regulates glucose levels in the blood. In normal circumstances, insulin is produced in response to raised glucose levels after eating. It then promotes the absorption of glucose into the liver and muscle cells, where it is converted into energy. Insulin is essential in preventing the build-up of glucose, and in ensuring that the body's tissue and cells have sufficient amounts of glucose for optimal functioning. Failing to produce insulin can lead to serious conditions such as diabetes. (See also **SUGAR**, **JUICING**, **POTASSIUM** and **ZINC**.)

INTOLERANCE/ALLERGY

When people experience symptoms such as bloating, constipation, diarrhoea or irritable bowel syndrome, they often put it down to an intolerance or allergy. In fact, this is unlikely. Genuine food intolerances and allergies are not common and tests for them can be unreliable. More than 1 in 5 Brits claims to have a food allergy or intolerance, an increase of 400 per cent in the past 20 years. However, research conducted by Portsmouth University has shown that of all those claiming to have an allergy or intolerance, only 2 per cent actually do. Similarly, across Europe, the Allergen Bureau

a b c d e f g h **i** j k l m n o p q r s t u v w x y z

estimates that despite 30 per cent of adult Europeans claiming to experience adverse food reactions, only 3–5 per cent have been diagnosed with a genuine allergy.

Around the world, millions of people have decided, or have been persuaded, that they are allergic to certain foods, the most popular culprit being wheat. In fact, the most common genuine allergens are peanuts, shellfish, eggs and soya; these serious allergies can have fatal consequences, but are mercifully rare. Between 2012 and 2014, sales of gluten-free products increased by 63 per cent – although surveys have found that most consumers do not actually know what gluten is or where it is found. Far from being healthier, gluten-free products may be full of other 'nasties': gluten-free bread, biscuits and cereal, for example, often contain refined ingredients such as additives, flavourings, stabilizers, added sugar and preservatives.

Recent years have seen an increase in the marketing of 'free-from' alternatives and a rise in the number of companies and private practitioners offering to diagnose and treat intolerances with unscientific testing kits. The media now regularly publish scare stories about the health dangers of eating certain foods. These are often alarmist and inaccurate – burnt toast and roast potatoes, for example, were recently linked to an increased cancer risk. This contributes to an uncertain climate around food, whereby people become confused about what they should and should not be eating. It may also lead to more orthorexic thinking, when anxieties around normal food morph into restrictive eating behaviours. Intolerance may then be a form of avoidance: someone who is trying to cut out carbohydrates claims to be wheat intolerant, for example.

If you suspect you may have a genuine intolerance, consult your GP or a registered dietitian. They will be able to make an accurate diagnosis based on an exclusion and reintroduction process, which is the most reliable method for testing for intolerance. They will also provide important advice to avoid dietary deficiencies: for example, if you are lactose intolerant and avoiding cow's milk, soya milk provides better protein and calcium than almond, oat or other plant milks. A genuine gluten intolerance might indicate something more serious such as coeliac disease, which needs medical supervision.

Don't waste money on expensive testing kits, and don't self-diagnose. It's important to have expert guidance before radically altering your diet or excluding whole food groups.

INTUITIVE EATING

See **MINDFUL EATING**.

IODINE

Iodine is a trace element in the body necessary for the production of the thyroid hormone. The thyroid gland, among other things, regulates the body's metabolism. Iodine deficiency leads to hypothyroidism, or underactive thyroid, which then causes the body's entire metabolism to slow down. During pregnancy, iodine deficiency can also be harmful to the developing baby. The body does not make its own iodine, so it is essential to get enough in the diet. Iodine is found in various foods, including dairy products, seafood, meat, some bread, eggs and iodized table salt, or by taking a multivitamin containing iodine.

IRON

As well as being the most common element on earth, iron is an essential mineral in the human body. It is vital for healthy growth and development, and plays a critical role in transferring oxygen around the body. Iron is distributed around the body via haemoglobin in red blood cells, myoglobin in the muscles, and in tissues, bone marrow, blood proteins, enzymes and plasma. Iron plays a crucial role in electron activity throughout the body, in keeping our immune system strong and in extracting energy from our food. Iron also helps muscles to function, and keeps our hair and skin in good condition. The average human male has around 4 g of iron in his body, and the average human female about 3.5 g.

The most bioavailable (easily absorbed) food sources of iron are red meats such as liver, beef and lamb, known as 'haem' sources of iron. Clams, molluscs, mussels and oysters are also rich in iron.

For vegetarians, 'non-haem' (plant-based) sources of iron include kidney beans, dark green leafy vegetables, soya beans, lentils, tofu, dried figs and apricots, molasses and brewer's yeast. Plant-based sources of iron are harder for the body to absorb than 'haem' or meat sources. However, vitamin C is a strong promoter of iron absorption, and when vitamin-C-rich foods are combined with foods rich in iron, absorption of iron is substantially increased.

The body regulates iron levels carefully, absorbing what it needs from food and storing any extra (mainly in the bone marrow and liver). Iron deficiency is fairly common, usually due to blood loss, increased iron requirements during childhood or growth periods or dietary deficiencies. Low iron levels are therefore most common in women (because of menstruation), pregnant women, very young children and the elderly. Some studies have shown that the majority of women in the UK do not reach the recommended daily intake of iron. Iron deficiency anaemia is straightforward to diagnose and treat. Symptoms may include weakness and fatigue, pale complexion, breathlessness or an increased number of infections (see **ANAEMIA**).

Too high levels of iron are rare, but can be problematic too, as the body has no way to dispose of extra iron. See your doctor for a simple blood test before you start taking iron supplements, as it's important to take the right amount and not too much.

ISOLATION

See **LONELINESS**.

j

JOURNAL

Many individuals with eating disorders struggle to verbalize their most intense feelings, even to close friends. Disordered eating becomes a way of coping or suppressing painful emotions: over-eating, purging or restricting may become reflex behaviours when thoughts or feelings are unmanageable. There are various ways you might tackle these challenging periods without resorting to self-harm: speaking to your therapist, ringing a friend or finding an activity that distracts you from food anxieties. Another method is to keep a regular journal or diary.

Shame, anger or self-disgust are quite common reactions to the illness, and writing this down can really help. It not only distracts you from the urge to binge or purge, but in addition helps you to process the overwhelming emotions. It can also help you and your therapist to identify triggers: perhaps you always binge after an argument with your parents or you go for a long session at the gym to cope with the guilt when you feel you've eaten something 'bad'. Learning to understand what you are doing and why can help you gain perspective on the situation. It will help you formulate different ways of reacting to similar situations in the future. No one can avoid all conflict, but we can find less harmful ways of coping.

Unfortunately, in anorexia and bulimia harmful behaviours can feel cathartic: people say they feel better after a punishing workout or lighter and cleaner after purging. People who cut themselves report feeling a sense of release. Keeping a diary is a good replacement for these damaging behaviours, because the act of 'writing out' your feelings gets them out of your head.

Your journal could cover daily ups and downs, experiences, even dreams – or it could focus specifically on your eating patterns. Many therapists and doctors recommend keeping a food diary. Writing down what you are going to eat (and what you have eaten) brings order to chaotic eating behaviours. Writing down what you feel before a binge episode can help identify when and why you are bingeing, and in time it may diffuse the feelings before an episode occurs. In anorexia, it can be reassuring to see things planned out. It also clarifies somatic sensations such as thirst and hunger. It may highlight specific foods you tend to binge on or behaviours at different times of the day.

Whatever the eating disorder, the prospect of food triggers a sort of red mist or panic. You may feel fearful or out of control. The very act of putting these feelings into words is calming, and can help you get a handle on your emotions.

Your journal or food diary can be private or you may decide to share it with your therapist. It might be written in list form, in pictures or in random words, however you communicate best. The only rule is *total honesty*: write down what you are really feeling, what you really ate, and then what you did after eating. At first it might seem silly or self-indulgent, but give yourself total freedom and honesty – if someone made a comment that upset you or you saw a friend's Instagram's post that made you feel inadequate, for example, or anything that matters to you. Don't spend too much time going back over previous posts, and don't self-censor.

Keeping this kind of diary can be painful, but it's an opportunity for you to understand and learn from the eating disorder. It can be a valuable outlet. Instead of suppressing emotions, you're allowing yourself to express them.

Over time, your diary will help you to build up a picture of what's happening in your head and why. A journal can be a safe place to express all your various emotions and get them out of your head – write them down, then put it aside and move on with your day. (See also **COGNITIVE BEHAVIOURAL THERAPY** and **COPING STRATEGIES**.)

JUICING

Juicers and blenders have become as ubiquitous as spiralizers in fashionable kitchens, and the recent explosion of juicing appears unquestionably healthy, although it may not be all that it seems. In fact, juicing can be as nutritionally suspect as other aspects of the clean eating movement, and is often the first step on the road to orthorexic-style disordered eating. Instead of simply consuming our five daily recommended portions of fruit and vegetables, we now find Instagram awash with the green juices of the rich and the beautiful, and juice bars and cafés charging hefty prices for their cold-pressed kale, spirulina and spinach concoctions.

However, most nutritionists agree that we should *eat* our fruit and vegetables, rather than drink them. Numerous studies have shown that drinking fruit juice can be as damaging to health as drinking fizzy drinks. For example, the rise in blood sugar that occurs after drinking apple juice is much higher than after eating an apple. The reason is simple: juicing destroys the important insoluble fibre in fruit, so the body is bombarded with high levels of the natural sugar fructose. The liver then struggles to deal with the excess fructose and converts it to liver fat, increasing the likelihood of insulin resistance, diabetes and heart disease.

From the perspective of eating disorders, juicing can be unhealthy – and downright unhelpful. For individuals prone to binge-eating or those trying to get down to a safe body weight, juicing appears a deceptively 'healthy' habit. But in fact juicing your fruit makes it very easy to overconsume. When is the last time you ate three apples, two bananas and a pack of strawberries all in one go? Yet when juiced, this quantity of fresh fruit is easy to drink, giving you around 20 teaspoons of sugar in a single hit (minus the healthy fibre in whole fruit that slows down digestion and satiates). When you bite, chew and swallow fruit and vegetables, the body registers that it is being fed, but when you drink them in the form of a juice, it does not.

For those who are underweight and exercising excessively, drinking fruit or vegetable juices is no substitute for eating solid foods. The entire process of digestion is bypassed on a liquid diet, leading to impaired stomach, bowel and digestive functioning. Drinking acidic juices also strips tooth enamel and leads to dental decay. This is particularly damaging for those with bulimia, who already risk dental problems due to repeated vomiting.

If you enjoy fruit and vegetable juices or struggle to eat your five-a-day, it's better to make your own. Shop-bought juices, even those that claim to be 100 per cent natural, are usually heat-treated or pasteurized, which destroys a large proportion of the vitamins, minerals and plant enzyme activity. For the price of a single juice-bar drink you can buy plenty of fresh fruit and veg – and it will ensure that you don't inadvertently consume extra sugars and preservatives. Even so, remember, juices should be an occasional treat, not a regular substitute for solid food or a supplement to every meal.

k

KETOSIS

Ketones are natural chemical products of fat metabolism, and ketosis is a natural part of the metabolic process. However, when there is insufficient glucose for the body to use as an energy source, ketosis can be a potentially serious condition. In ketosis, the body burns stored fats instead of regular blood glucose (from carbohydrates), which results in the build-up of acids known as ketones in the blood. In the context of disordered eating, this form of nutritional ketosis may be the result of starvation, malnutrition or extreme low-carb dieting, when the body is forced into an accelerated fat-burning state. Diabetic ketosis is a related but equally serious condition.

Symptoms of ketosis include halitosis (low-carb eaters often report bad breath), lethargy or loss of appetite, nausea and abdominal pain. Untreated, the condition may lead to confusion, loss of consciousness and death. When mild ketosis is triggered by starving or fasting, it should respond well to improved nutrition, with no lasting damage.

KEYS' CLASSIC STUDY

The research carried out by the American scientist Ancel Keys in 1944 will be of interest to anyone affected by an eating disorder. Keys' Minnesota Starvation Experiment is considered to be one of the most authoritative studies on the physiological effects of self-starvation, providing valuable insight into how eating disorders develop.

Keys selected 36 healthy young men for his research study. None of them had any kind of unhealthy body image, preoccupation with food or weight or known mental disorders.

During the first three months of the experiment, the men ate normally, while their behaviour, personality and eating patterns were studied in detail. Over the next six months, the men were restricted to approximately half of their former calorie intake. During this semi-starvation phase, they lost, on average, 25 per cent of their former weight.

The first change observed in the men was a dramatic increase in food preoccupations. They thought about eating constantly and struggled to concentrate on anything else. Food became their principal topic of conversation, reading and daydreams. As their obsessive food thoughts increased, there was a corresponding decline in interest in all their usual activities.

As starvation progressed, the men's behaviour at mealtimes changed. They reported conflicting desires to bolt their food ravenously or consume it slowly in order to prolong the sensations of taste and smell. They smuggled food out of the dining room, read cookbooks and recipes obsessively, collected kitchen utensils, even rummaged through rubbish bins and hoarded random scraps. This tendency to hoard has also been observed in starved anorexic patients and even in rats deprived of food.

Although the men were psychologically healthy prior to the experiment, they experienced significant emotional deterioration as a result of semi-starvation. Some developed severe depression and psychosis – one man cut three fingers off his own hand. They also exhibited many physical changes, including gastrointestinal discomfort, insomnia, dizziness, headaches, hypersensitivity to noise and light, reduced strength, poor motor control, oedema, hair loss, decreased tolerance for cold temperatures, visual and auditory disturbances, and **PARAESTHESIA** – all classic symptoms of anorexia nervosa.

The men's personalities changed too. Originally outgoing and sociable, they became progressively more withdrawn and isolated. Humour and comradeship diminished, and feelings of inadequacy increased. The men became totally uninterested in pursuing any kind of romantic or sexual relationships with women.

After the six-month semi-starvation period, the men were placed on a refeeding programme, but the problems continued:

> Subject #20 stuffs himself until he is bursting at the seams, to the point of being nearly sick and still feels hungry; #120 reported that he had to discipline himself to keep from eating so much as to become ill; subject #1 ate until he was uncomfortably full; and subject #30 had so little control over the mechanics of "piling it in" that he simply had to stay away from food because he could not find a point of satiation even when he was "full to the gills."
> . . . "I ate practically all weekend," reported subject #26. "I would just as soon have eaten six meals instead of three."

Keys' study concluded that extreme psychological changes had taken place in these men. Even while they were gradually being restored to a healthy weight, they were unable to recover from their obsession with food. Their bodies never got over that period of starvation and their minds were permanently hardwired to think there was never enough food – they had to eat, eat, eat or they would starve to death.

It is crucial to remember that these were psychologically and physically healthy young men. And yet many of the symptoms once thought to be primary features of anorexia nervosa, neurosis and body-image anxiety are simply symptoms of starvation itself.

KIDNEYS

These are two organs situated at the back of the abdominal cavity, on either side of the spine. They filter blood and excrete waste products and water as urine. The kidneys regulate fluid balance in the body, and are involved in hormonal production of red blood cells and maintenance of blood pressure.

Behaviours such as self-induced vomiting in bulimia nervosa may result in kidney dysfunction. This is thought to be related to chronic hypokalaemia (low potassium) or excessive fluid loss, usually due to severe diarrhoea, vomiting or use of diuretics. Kidney complications can lead to frequent urinary tract infections and, in severe cases, long-term kidney damage.

KLEPTOMANIA

This is the recurring and overwhelming impulse to steal objects, often without the desire or need for the actual object itself. The stolen objects are usually of little monetary value or use to the individual, and in most cases they could afford to buy them. Stolen items may be hoarded or stashed away, given to friends or even discarded.

Kleptomania differs from shoplifting as the individual does not steal for personal gain but is unable to control the behaviour. Kleptomania is classified as an impulse control disorder, which means that individuals have difficulty resisting the temptation to perform an act that is excessive or harmful to themselves or to someone else. Kleptomaniacs report a feeling of tension before the theft and a sense of release or calm afterwards. They may also feel self-loathing and intense guilt. Urges to steal may come and go, depending on their other conditions or mental health.

Since kleptomania was first identified in 1816, it has been associated with a range of other mental illnesses, including bipolar disorder, anxiety disorder, substance abuse and mood/personality disorders. It is also a surprisingly common feature of eating disorders. The connections between kleptomania and eating disorders are not fully understood, but compulsive stealing is seen in individuals with bulimia and BED. These conditions are marked by problems with risk-taking, impulse control, anxiety and depression. Stealing seems to relieve the anxiety, temporarily, in the same way as a binge-eating or binge–purge episode.

Kleptomania is estimated to have a worldwide prevalence of around 0.6 per cent, of which approximately two-thirds are female. However, as with other antisocial behaviours, the stigma associated with stealing makes any accurate estimate impossible. People are not only ashamed but also frightened of admitting their criminal behaviour, even to a therapist.

New research on kleptomania has highlighted possible neuro-chemical imbalances, specifically in relation to the neurotransmitter serotonin. Serotonin helps to regulate moods and emotions, and low levels of serotonin are common in people prone to impulsive behaviours. Acting on kleptomaniac urges may trigger the release of dopamine, a neurotransmitter that causes pleasurable feelings. Treating the chemical imbalances with SSRIs, mood stabilizers or opioid agonists can be highly effective in individuals with klepto-mania. These drugs are often used alongside conventional CBT and support groups.

1

LANGUAGE

You may think that what you *say*, what you *do* and how you *feel* are all separate, but in fact they are closely interrelated. The words we use about ourselves contribute to the way we feel about ourselves, especially when it comes to our bodies. The language of body image is often shockingly self-critical – not only for people with eating disorders, but also for women in general. Tactical beauty commercials remind us of physical 'flaws' and tell us we should cover up, conceal or blur our 'imperfections', transform our bodies, dye our hair, and turn back the clock.

We routinely use terms of hatred about our own bodies that we would not dream of using about the bodies of others. Muffin tops, bingo wings, thunder thighs, fat cow, flabby bitch – this casually abusive language undermines our confidence on a daily basis. So why not clean up your language? Ban the unkind self-talk and treat your body with respect. Replace the automatic negative thoughts with some positive thoughts at the start of every day. Don't fixate on your perceived problem areas, and don't obsess over the mirror or the bathroom scales.

Try to appreciate difference. Perhaps you're tall or tiny, pale-skinned or dark, have a long nose or small hands – these basic characteristics will be with you for life. You appreciate the physical quirks that make others unique, so why not appreciate your own? Think of your friends who are different sizes. How would you describe their body shapes: sporty, slender, hourglass? Find some language of positivity for your own body too, instead of self-hatred.

Another great way to improve your inner body image is to change your attitude: focus on what your body *does*, rather than how it *looks*. Think about the muscles and bones that enable you to walk and run; the skin that keeps you clean and dry; the brain cells that enable you to communicate and dream; the nerves that allow you to touch and hold. When you accept that your body is a miraculously functioning physical machine, you are more able to listen to its needs for food and rest, to eat healthily and well, instead of damaging it with starving and bingeing. That process begins with thoughts and words and attitude: what you *say* about your body really does change the way you *feel*. (See also **BODY IMAGE**.)

LANUGO

This soft, pale, downy hair is common on fetuses and newborn babies, but is also a feature of severe anorexia. The individual with anorexia struggles to preserve body heat, due to lack of subcutaneous fat, poor circulation and a very low intake of caloric energy. The growth of lanugo is the body's attempt to insulate itself when it is malnourished and emaciated.

Lanugo usually grows on the arms, back and chest, sometimes the face, and resembles a peach fuzz. While newborn babies shed their lanugo soon before or after birth, anorexic lanugo persists as long as the individual remains underweight. When good nutrition is established and body weight is restored, the lanugo should gradually disappear.

LAPSES

When relapses occur, as they will, stay calm. Don't catastrophize and don't blame yourself. Remember that every recovery involves setbacks. (Read books on successful businessmen, who all recommend failure as the best way to success!) Getting over an addiction as serious as an eating disorder is tough, and there will be lapses along the way. In anorexia, perhaps you are aiming to buy new foods at the supermarket, then you panic, dump the shopping basket and flee the shop. In bulimia, you might be doing everything you can to avoid a late-night binge, but then you find yourself bingeing on 'danger' foods and end up making yourself sick. These are common experiences in recovery from an eating disorder and entirely understandable. Many, many others have gone through exactly the same setbacks, you are not greedy or weak, and you're not alone. Be gentle with your body and mind, as you relearn how and what and when to eat. Remind yourself of the reasons you want to recover: write down your feelings if this helps, and talk to a friend or your counsellor.

Above all, don't let a relapse knock you off course. Research shows that the more attempts someone makes to overcome an addiction (drugs, nicotine or alcohol), the more likely they are to succeed eventually. Use lapses as part of the learning process: ask yourself what triggered the episode – stress, upset, anger or boredom? What might help next time, and how can you get back on track?

LATE ONSET

Eating disorders have long been associated with teenagers and younger adults, with anorexia and bulimia considered primarily diseases of the young. The ages of 12 to 20 years are viewed as the riskiest times for the development of disordered eating. However, it is becoming clear that adolescence is not the only transitional period in our lives – middle age can present challenges too. Anyone can be vulnerable at any time, and the pressures appear to be increasing across the age range.

A study in 2017 reported that a 'significant' number of women in their 40s and 50s had an active eating disorder. Researchers from University College London studied over 5000 middle-aged women in the UK and found that 15 per cent of them had experienced an eating disorder at some point in their lifetime, and that 3.6 per cent were currently affected. The study was the first time that prevalence had been investigated in a population of women in their fifth and sixth decades. The study uncovered both chronic and late-onset cases, showing that eating disorders can last for years or can actually begin in middle age.

These figures are higher than previously thought, with national headlines describing it as a 'hidden epidemic'. This is, however, also due to the increased awareness of eating disorders in middle age and among the elderly. In part, this is down to increased awareness within the medical and psychiatric community: as we understand more about these complex conditions, they can be more easily diagnosed in middle-aged and older people. It may also be down to increased media pressures on women and men of all ages to carry on looking great, staying in shape and being slim and fit well into middle age and later life (see also **ELDERLY**).

Women in particular face intense pressures to 'have it all', juggling family, careers, social life and domestic duties, often during a period of personal change, while still remaining youthful and attractive. It is clear that many of the biopsychosocial factors that were previously thought to affect teenagers also affect older women: low self-esteem, body-image anxiety and perfectionism, as well as pressure to look like the superwomen they see in magazines and online, and to conform to society's ideal of female beauty. All of these render them vulnerable to eating disorders.

There are also pressures that are specific to middle age, a time of considerable transition. Middle-aged women must contend with approaching menopause and anxieties around ageing, which can lead to anxiety, depression and negative body image. They may be more vulnerable because of hormonal changes, weight gain due to menopause, and their core beliefs about fertility and their own value as mothers and sexual partners. They may also feel 'out of control' as their body changes, leaving them at greater risk of using dis-ordered eating as a coping mechanism. Divorce, financial and career pressures, bereavement and empty nest syndrome may also trigger restrictive eating, bingeing or other forms of self-harm.

Another crucial factor in late-onset eating disorders is that individuals may have been suffering in silence for decades. In the 2017 research, under 30 per cent of the middle-aged women with an eating disorder said they had sought help. Women and men with mild to moderate anorexia or bulimia may have never admitted to their problems and never have been treated or they may have relapsed from earlier difficulties. The worrying phenomenon known as SEED (severe and enduring eating disorders) stores up many health problems for those with eating disorders in older age – osteoporosis, for example, in very underweight older women, and diabetes and other obesity-related conditions in older binge-eaters.

BED may develop out of an earlier or pre-existing problem, for example among those who have had anorexia or bulimia as young people. BED is more common among middle-aged and older people who are alone or are experiencing depression or social isolation. They have the time and money to buy large quantities of food, and may feel that no one cares any more what they look like. They may have spent years cooking and caring for a family, for example, and feel a loss of purpose without anyone to look after. For many different reasons, disordered eating can become a way of coping with the unforeseen challenges of middle age.

LAXATIVES

Laxatives are used to loosen stools and stimulate bowel movements, and can be an effective solution for occasional constipation. They come in the form of tablets, powder, liquid and suppositories, and are widely available in supermarkets and pharmacies. However, they should only be taken occasionally and for short periods of time.

Excessive laxative use is widespread in disordered eating, in an attempt to speed up the process of elimination and thus purge the body of calories. Prolonged use of laxatives can have serious health consequences. Signs of laxative abuse are similar to those of other secretive eating disorder behaviours: buying large quantities of the medication from different shops, hiding them from friends, concealing the problem from the doctor or therapist, increasing the amount taken, and feeling anxious when unable to take them.

The most immediate result of laxative abuse is constipation. This is because the bowel becomes 'lazy', relying on the laxatives to do its job. This leads to a worsening of constipation and induces the individual to take more laxatives. The result is a vicious cycle (see **CONSTIPATION**): the more laxatives taken, the more disrupted bowel functioning becomes, which only exacerbates the original constipation.

It should be noted that laxatives are in fact very ineffective as a purgative. The body absorbs calories in food surprisingly quickly, and it is estimated that laxatives dispose of only 12 per cent of the calories ingested. The individual may believe that he or she has lost weight, but this is largely water loss. Because of this, laxatives can cause dehydration, as well as fainting, stomach pains and diarrhoea (and in such cases, medical help should be sought).

Laxative abuse can cause serious long-term damage, such as permanent impairment of bowel functioning. Nerve cells in the bowel may degenerate, and surgery may be required. However, in most cases, bowel function should return to normal with time and patience: the essential step is to stop taking the laxatives. The best way to do this is through gradual lifestyle changes: re-establishing regular eating patterns, including natural fibre in your diet and drinking plenty of water. Apricots, figs and prunes are healthy natural sources of fibre, as are most other fruit and vegetables and soluble fibres such as porridge and oat bran.

LETTING GO

Letting go means something different to each of us. It could be letting go of bitterness and regret, letting go of comparing yourself to others. It could be letting go of self-limiting beliefs, painful memories or experiences, difficult family relationships or failed love affairs. We persist in harmful habits – smoking, overeating or drinking – because it's easier to stay stuck than it is to change. One of the most harmful of these is disordered eating, which damages us and holds us back. If you let go of your eating disorder, what might happen?

There is a beautiful mantra, 'Let go. You were never in control anyway.' It might just help you to challenge the routines you're stuck in, embrace change and let go. (See also **IMPROMPTU**.)

LIBIDO

See **SEX**.

LIES

See **DISHONESTY**.

LONELINESS

All mental illness involves some degree of loneliness: you are ill inside your head so it's hard for others to understand what you're going through. Most mental illness involves depression too, when the impulse to avoid others isolates you further. Eating disorders, however, have an added layer of loneliness that outsiders cannot understand and often misinterpret. That is, that eating is an inherently social activity. Food brings people together, as couples, colleagues or families. All significant occasions are marked with shared meals; breaking bread together is an ancient human ritual.

When you live with severely disordered eating, these social get-togethers are fraught with peril. In anorexia, the fear is of being forced to eat, being confronted with unsafe foods, being watched. In bulimia or BED, the fear might be of losing control and eating too much or not being able to purge afterwards or being stared at. Eating in secret is not only isolating, but also leads to many misunderstandings. Outsiders assume you are unfriendly or stand-offish if you don't join in; colleagues may wonder why you don't go for lunch with them; a potential partner may be offended if you turn down an invitation to dinner. Not being able to eat 'normally' in public with others causes both practical problems and anxiety.

One of the best things you can do for those with eating disorders is to include them. Be sensitive to their eating issues, and invite them for a coffee or a walk instead. This is not to say that they do not need to challenge their eating difficulties – they do – but meanwhile, the loneliness can be extreme.

MAGNESIUM

This abundant mineral is essential to almost all of the body's complex biochemical reactions. It is involved in metabolism, enzyme function, bone structure, protein synthesis, energy production and nerve impulses. It regulates blood glucose and blood pressure, transports calcium and potassium ions across cell membranes, and ensures normal heart rhythm. It also has a critical role in muscle function: without magnesium, our muscles would be in a permanent state of contraction. The average adult body contains around 25 g of magnesium, over 50 per cent of which is stored in our bones – making it hard to measure magnesium levels from routine blood tests.

Eating a lot of sugary foods, a high intake of carbonated drinks, alcohol and caffeine consumption and being ill or under stress or elderly – among many other factors – are all thought to deplete magnesium levels. US studies have reported that less than 30 per cent of adults reach their daily recommended intake of magnesium. Symptoms of low magnesium intake can include muscle cramps or spasms, facial tics, chronic pain and poor sleep. Inadequate magnesium has also been associated with osteoporosis (see **OSTEOPOROSIS/OSTEOPENIA**), so it is crucial for all women, especially those who are underweight, to consume enough magnesium.

Good food sources include dark green leafy vegetables, legumes, nuts, seeds, fish, beans and whole grains, yogurt, avocado, bananas, dried fruit and dark chocolate. In general, foods containing dietary fibre provide magnesium. Magnesium is also added to some breakfast cereals and other fortified foods. As always, eating a naturally magnesium-rich diet is preferable to supplementation because of the delicate interaction with other elements, which can be upset by excessive doses. The metabolism of magnesium is connected to other nutrients within the body, including calcium, vitamin K and vitamin D.

MALES

Although eating disorders have traditionally been seen as female conditions, an increasing number of men are affected too. The precise figures for men (as for women) are unreliable, because of the stigma around these issues. It is likely that numbers are considerably higher than estimated as many individuals with disordered eating never seek medical help or are not deemed 'ill enough' for treatment, while others are treated privately. The official NHS statistics only record the numbers of patients treated in NHS hospitals or inpatient clinics and, as such, underestimate the prevalence of disordered eating. The general consensus of UK organizations such as the National Institute for Health and Care Excellence (NICE) and Department of Health is that approximately 11 per cent of those with eating disorders are male, although B-EAT (the UK's leading eating disorders charity) suggests that up to 25 per cent of those affected could be male.

There is still a stigma for men in admitting to a condition that is perceived to be effeminate or unmanly. In addition, doctors, teachers and parents may fail to identify warning signs in boys that they would immediately recognize in girls: concern over body weight and shape, distress around eating or secretive behaviours around food. Partly due to this lack of awareness by the health professions, boys and men are even more ashamed of coming forward than women and girls.

Male eating disorders are most likely to begin between the ages of 14 and 25 years, but just like women, men of any age can develop them. While society is starting to acknowledge the pressures on older women to stay thin (see **ELDERLY** and **LATE ONSET**), we rarely think about older men.

Comparatively little research has been carried out on male eating disorders. It is clear, however, that many of the risk factors which apply to women apply to men too, in particular the use of dieting or bingeing as a coping mechanism or an expression of underlying emotional stress. Men face a heightened risk if they have previously been overweight or obesity or eating disorders run in their family. Like women, men with anorexia tend to conform to a particular personality type: anxious, obsessive, persevering and perfectionist. They tend to be eager to please and sensitive to rejection and humiliation.

Men are also more susceptible if they participate in sports that demand a particular body build, whether large or small. Runners and jockeys seem to show a higher prevalence of anorexia and bulimia. Wrestlers who try to shed pounds quickly before a bout in order to compete in a lower weight category can also be vulnerable. Bodybuilders are at risk if they deplete body fat and fluid reserves to achieve high muscle definition, as are male models who fast or starve themselves to hone the 'ripped' look seen on the covers of men's magazines.

Research suggests that eating disorders disproportionately affect some segments of the LGBT population, specifically gay and bisexual men. Gay men are thought to represent only a few per cent of the total male population, but among men who have eating disorders, somewhere between 20 and 40 per cent identify as gay. In one study, gay males were 7 times more likely to report bingeing and 12 times more likely to report purging than heterosexual males.

According to the National Eating Disorder Association, 'eating disorders among LGBT populations should be understood within the broader cultural context of oppression.' While one cannot generalize as to why the gay and bisexual male community is at particular risk, a number of factors appear to be relevant. The most significant is the experience of being young and gay, with intense anxiety about coming out, fear of rejection by friends and family, social isolation and discrimination within the workplace. Even today, gay men encounter prejudice and even violence: a significant proportion of male anorexics report bullying over their sexuality at school.

Body image ideals within the gay community may also contribute: it is suggested that attractiveness and appearance pressures in terms of slimness and the 'perfect body', similar to the pressures on women within the heterosexual community, may cause more body-image disturbance and dissatisfaction among gay men.

Whatever a man's sexuality, male eating disorders are damaging and dangerous. Disorders last on average eight years in men, a third longer than in women. Treatment options for male eating disorders are improving, but they are still limited, with most clinics and hospital units set up for females. The focus on women's health issues, menstruation and female body image is highly alienating for young men battling the same condition, and can reinforce the message that they have a girl's problem. In fact, men face significant health risks from restricting, bingeing and purging. (See also **BIGOREXIA**.)

MELATONIN

Melatonin is a hormone secreted by the pineal gland, a small gland found deep in the centre of the brain. It maintains the body's circadian rhythms, which control the body's natural sleep–wake cycles (as well as regulating reproductive hormones).

Melatonin is an important precursor for sleep. When eating habits are disrupted, so are sleep patterns. Sleeping pills are never a long-term solution, but certain foods are known to promote the release of melatonin, so include these in your evening meal or as a bedtime snack. Turkey and lettuce contain tryptophan, the precursor of melatonin. Honey contains orexin, which reduces alertness. Marmite, almonds and oatcakes make good night-time snacks, as do bananas, as they contain high levels of serotonin and magnesium. Camomile and warm milk are sleep-inducing bedtime drinks.

MENSTRUATION

See **AMENORRHOEA**.

METABOLISM

This is the collective term for all the chemical processes that occur within the body's cells by which nutrients are converted into energy and build new tissues and repair cells. Metabolism is divided into two different processes: the breaking down of complex substances into simple ones, known as catabolism, and the building up of complex substances from simple ones, known as anabolism. Catabolism is the process that releases energy; anabolism is the process that uses it. The energy needed to keep the body functioning at rest is known as the basal metabolic rate, measured in joules or kilocalories. This basal metabolic rate increases in response to a wide range of factors, such as activity and exertion, stress and fear, temperature and illness.

The metabolism responds to anorexia by slowing down. When it is starved of nutrition, it seeks to conserve its dwindling energy reserves in order to keep the body going. When you undernourish your body, the speed of weight loss will decrease. Similar to famine conditions, the body seeks to burn calories at a slower rate to preserve vital organs and tissues, and maintain basic functioning of the brain, kidneys, liver and so on. As the metabolic rate slows right down, growth slows, menstruation stops (see **AMENORRHOEA**) and feelings of weakness, cold and fatigue increase. This state of malnutrition means there is simply not enough fuel in the metabolic tank.

MINDFUL EATING

Also known as intuitive eating, this can be a good way out of the endless cycle of crash dieting, weight loss and weight gain in which many overeaters find themselves. It is also a powerful strategy for those who are undereating or underweight, because it takes the guilt out of eating.

Eating intuitively or mindfully means no rules, no fad diets and no calorie counting. Mind*ful* eating is the opposite of mind*less* eating, when you eat out of boredom, stress or anxiety. In mindful, or intuitive, eating, all foods are allowed and no foods are forbidden.

So, if you want a slice of cake for breakfast, you can have it. You don't get overweight from eating a slice of cake, because you won't always want cake – and when you don't deprive yourself, you don't crave fattening foods. You take time to savour your food, slow down and chew every mouthful, notice the colours and textures. You don't eat while working or chatting on the phone. You don't eat while in a highly emotional state, and you don't use food as a reward or punishment. Intuitive eating works on the principle of trusting yourself and honouring your appetite. When you listen to what your body is asking for, you find that sometimes it wants healthy food, and sometimes it wants a treat. Best of all, you avoid the emotional eating trap familiar to many of us. (See also **HUNGER**.)

MODERATION

See **BALANCE**.

MOOD

As we've seen, the brain is a hungry organ: it uses around 50 per cent of the body's blood sugar supply even at rest. In order to function properly – to think and study and recall and communicate – the brain needs regular refuelling. When this supply of fuel is restricted or erratic, as in disordered eating, the brain struggles to cope. This is why disordered eating has such an impact on an individual's mood and emotions, and appears to change their normal personality.

Put simply, food affects the brain, and different nutrients, or lack of nutrients, affect the brain in different ways. Fat, for example, makes up 60 per cent of the dry weight of the brain: this explains why following a very low-fat diet can cause low mood and depression. The brain's electrical signals and impulses control messages going all around the human body, and they require vitamins, minerals and other nutritional fuel to function properly. Many of the brain's naturally occurring chemicals are derived from food, and they all have a role to play in our mood and our ability to learn and think clearly.

Research into eating disorders tends to focus on the physical damage associated with starving, bingeing, vomiting or laxative abuse. However, the personal, emotional and social upheaval of continually hiding, avoiding other people and eating or starving secretly is just as devastating. Individuals may become withdrawn, depressed, angry or aggressive, secretive or dishonest. These changes are usually temporary, but they clearly demonstrate that eating disorders affect the mind just as much as the body. Indeed, they affect every aspect of your relationship with others and with yourself.

Approximately 25 per cent of people experience some form of mood disturbance during their lifetime. Women are more commonly affected than men, perhaps because of their regular monthly hormonal cycles. Neurotransmitters in the brain play a significant role in our mood and in mood disorders. We have looked at the key neurotransmitters: dopamine and noradrenaline, the motivational neurotransmitters that help us feel alert and energized, and serotonin, the feel-good neurotransmitter that helps us feel happy and calm. These chemical messengers are made from amino acids, found in protein, and from carbohydrate and other substances in the food we eat. Tryptophan-rich proteins and carbohydrates, for example, are considered to be especially mood-enhancing, hence the term 'comfort food'. These proteins and carbohydrates are just as essential as fat to the brain, providing yet more proof that our diet directly affects how we feel.

As well as their different hormone levels, women have naturally lower levels of serotonin than men. Research has found that women who follow a low-carbohydrate diet for weight loss, such as Atkins or Dukan, experience increased irritability and unsteady moods. Eating good-quality carbohydrates is essential for a slow supply of glucose into the bloodstream, which is needed for a steady release of serotonin to moderate and stabilize the mood (see **SEROTONIN**).

Mood swings, feelings of despair or hopelessness, emotional over-reactions, aggression and clinical depression are common in eating disorders. Some of this is down to social isolation and frustration; some is due to the brain struggling to cope with inadequate nutrition.

The body may also be coping with lack of sleep, constant anxiety and extreme hunger.

Emotional instability and mood swings can be hard to control and upsetting to family, friends and colleagues. However, there is no evidence to suggest that these personality changes are permanent. The emotional instability caused by eating disorders is temporary and reversible, when good nutrition and a healthy body weight are restored. When you are deep in an eating disorder, it seems impossible that food could solve anything. But never underestimate just how soothing, calming and comforting a square meal can be. (See also **PERSONALITY/PERSONALITY TRAITS**.)

MOTIVATION

It is essential to find your personal motivation to recover. This should not be just health reasons – although they are vitally important – but an individual and compelling reason why YOU want to get better. It doesn't need to be groundbreaking or world-changing, but it must matter to you. It could be going to college, being able to pursue your dream job or travel the world. It may be that you want to meet a life partner and your eating disorder is holding you back or you want to be well enough to have a baby. Whatever your individual motivation, remind yourself of it every day – surround yourself with positive images, sticky notes, affirmations and mantras! Find the thing you really want, and use it to power your recovery.

MYTHS AND MISUNDERSTANDINGS

Eating disorders are perhaps the most misunderstood of all mental illnesses. Despite growing research that now points to a neuro-biological basis, it is assumed, because the primary symptom is disordered eating, that the problem is simply about food and weight. Furthermore, because these disorders have such visible physical consequences, it is assumed that those with them are obsessed with their own physical appearance.

In fact, the roots of disordered eating lie in complex behavioural and psychological patterns, and possibly even neurological dysfunction. The focus on the body in relation to eating disorders can be highly misleading: the individuals may be concerned with their body weight and shape, but they may also be struggling with depression, anxiety, obsessions and compulsions, a need for control, childhood trauma or other emotional distress.

Added to this is our Western society's obsession with weight loss and idealization of thinness. The media coverage of high-profile female figures – actresses, singers, even politicians – invariably focuses on their appearance, with negative comments for weight gain and positive comments for weight loss. From fairy tales to celebrity magazines to their own mothers' diets, it's no wonder that little girls (and increasingly boys) grow up accepting that fat is bad and thin is good.

The reaction to eating disorders is also unhelpful and counter-productive. People are horrified by the extreme emaciation seen in anorexia or the extreme obesity sometimes seen in BED. The public reaction ranges from thinking that individuals with anorexia have only themselves to blame to envying their 'self-discipline' around food. Anorexic individuals can be labelled as 'narcissistic' or self-obsessed, and told to get over themselves. Binge-eaters are labelled as 'greedy' and told to get some self-control. Purging, especially vomiting, is met with incomprehension and disgust. In all cases, saying 'just eat less' or 'just eat more' is deeply unhelpful, since this is exactly what the individual cannot do. Anorexics do not 'choose' to starve themselves, just as those with bulimia do not 'choose' to submit their bodies to the damaging binge–purge cycle.

Casual assumptions and judgemental comments not only fail to address the underlying issues but are also hurtful to the individuals concerned. The wider social stigma of an eating disorder – the individuals' sense of being abnormal – intensifies their isolation. It exacerbates the secrecy and shame of eating disorders, and may prevent them from seeking help. In particular, social disapproval of obesity means that many binge-eaters hide their difficulties for many years. Being labelled as greedy or gluttonous reinforces the self-disgust they already feel, hence the high levels of anxiety and depression accompanying many of these conditions (see also **CO-MORBIDITY**).

Whereas there have been numerous studies on social stigma and other psychiatric conditions such as schizophrenia, bipolar disorder and depression, there have been fewer studies on the stigma of eating disorders. Nevertheless, in recent years the understanding of eating disorders has begun to improve. This is due to developments in neuroscience and more research into the biological, neurological and psychological causes of eating disorders. Increased media coverage and the sharing of personal stories have also contributed to greater understanding among the general public. Perhaps the most important shift in attitude has been the gradual acceptance that eating disorders are not volitional, that the individuals are not to 'blame' for their condition, and they need more than harsh words to get better.

n

NEUROSCIENCE

Neuroimaging techniques have revolutionized the understanding of eating disorders, allowing neuroscientists to look closely at specific brain regions in individuals with anorexia, bulimia and related conditions. The brain's complex cortical structures, neural pathways and neurotransmitters play a significant role in how every one of us thinks, feels and acts – and therefore in disordered eating behaviour. The possibility of a neurobiological basis to such conditions has greatly contributed to the diagnosis and treatment of eating disorders.

Neuroimaging techniques have enabled scientists to look at the neurological, cognitive and psychological effects of starvation and build up a clearer picture of how it affects the brain both during acute illness and afterwards. Are brain changes a result of extreme weight loss, and do they reverse afterwards?

Neuroscience has revealed important anatomical features such as cerebral atrophy – or brain shrinkage – in patients with anorexia compared with normal patients. Also, there is a reduction in grey matter (containing most of the brain's nerve cell bodies) and white matter (containing long projections of nerves that allow synaptic connections).

From this research, neuroscience has begun to shed light on more complex cognitive and behavioural difficulties commonly experienced in individuals with severe eating disorders. Impairments may include attention, memory, visuospatial processing, impulsivity and decision-making – and what is known as cognitive flexibility or 'set-shifting' (see **COGNITIVE IMPAIRMENT**). Clearly, these go well beyond the standard textbook symptoms of eating disorders such as body-image anxiety, desire for weight loss and avoidance of food.

The neuroscience research into eating disorders uses techniques such as computerized (or computed) tomography (CT), positron emission tomography (PET), magnetic resonance imaging (MRI), functional imaging and functional MRI (fMRI). Future research will explore brain structure, neurochemistry and functioning, providing a greater understanding of issues around vulnerability, heritability, triggers and possible genetic links in these complex conditions. This will contribute to the development of more effective psychological therapies (see **COGNITIVE REMEDIATION THERAPY**) and possibly pharmacological treatments targeted at specific areas of the brain.

NIGHT-EATING SYNDROME

This is a night-bingeing disorder thought to affect up to 1.5 per cent of the population. It is characterized by delayed circadian patterns of food intake that disrupt the person's normal functioning and sleep patterns. Individuals report a lack of appetite in the morning, extremely elevated appetite in the evening and recurrent night-time bingeing. In other words, they eat the majority of their daily calories in the evening and during the night. This leads to isolation and secrecy, mental distress and sleep disturbance.

Night-eating syndrome may be triggered by extreme dieting, where people try to restrict all day, or it could arise from something as simple as working night shifts. The individual may be of normal weight or overweight. Night-eating syndrome is not the same as BED, although night-eaters may have episodes of binge-eating too. Individuals with night-eating syndrome often display other eating disorder traits such as depression, anxiety and negative body image.

NORADRENALINE

This neurotransmitter, also known as norepinephrine, plays a key role in the brain's alertness, fight-or-flight and threat detection responses. Feelings of anxiety and panic are fuelled by noradrenaline circulating in the amygdala and sympathetic nervous system, the body's alarm system. Noradrenaline also helps to regulate healthy blood flow around the brain. Individuals with anorexia often display excessive or dysfunctional noradrenaline activity.

NOREPINEPHRINE

See **NORADRENALINE**.

NORMAL DIET

There is no such thing as a 'normal' diet. Each person needs different amounts of energy depending on age, work, metabolism, health and levels of physical activity. Every one of us has likes and dislikes for certain flavours, preferred times of day to eat, different beliefs and habits around food.

Nonetheless, individuals with disordered eating are often very concerned about how many calories is 'normal', what 'normal' people eat and what a 'normal' amount of food looks like. For this reason, general guidelines can be very helpful in reorientating them back into the mainstream, such as reminding those with anorexia that it's normal to eat three proper meals a day or reminding those with bulimia that it's not normal to bring up food after mealtimes. These basic facts sound obvious but can easily get lost in the world of chaotic, disordered eating.

A 'normal' diet looks something like this: around 2,000 calories a day. Women are advised to aim for between 1,800 and 2,200 calories (more if they are physically active), men to aim for 2,200–2,800 calories (again, depending on levels of activity). Daily calorie intake is normally divided into three main meals – breakfast, lunch and dinner – often with a snack mid-morning and mid-afternoon. A 'normal' diet includes carbohydrates, protein and fats, as well as the occasional treat. 'Normal' eating means not hiding or throwing away food, not cutting portions into tiny pieces, not eating in secret or purging afterwards. It means being able to enjoy meals in a social context without planning in advance or feeling panicky or out of control.

These days, the 'normal' diet is increasingly rare, with the popularity of intermittent fasting and so-called 5:2 style diets, as well as low-carb, raw-food or gluten-free regimes. This can make recovery from an eating disorder even harder. However, the concept of 'normal' – aiming for 2,000 calories a day, eating regularly and enjoying a broad range of different food – can be a useful road map for those who are severely restricting, purging or overeating.

NUTRITION

Individuals with eating disorders are often surprisingly well informed about nutrition. Clinicians report that their patients can recite the nutritional profile of any given food, spend a lot of time reading recipes and food magazines and follow many clean-eating blogs. It is ironic that individuals who are so well informed about nutrition should malnourish themselves. They may prepare elaborate meals for their family or bake cakes to give to friends – but very rarely eat themselves. As seen in the 1944 Minnesota Study (see **KEYS' CLASSIC STUDY**), such preoccupation with food is common among those who are deprived of it. Similarly, for those with anorexia, bulimia, orthorexia and other eating disorders, food is both fascinating and frightening. However, with time this interest in nutrition can also be turned into a positive tool for recovery.

OBESITY/OVERWEIGHT

According to the standard **BODY MASS INDEX (BMI)**, which is a measure of an individual's weight against height, individuals are overweight if their BMI exceeds 25, and obese if it exceeds 30.

Two-thirds of UK adults (67.8 per cent of men and 58.1 per cent of women) are overweight, and just over a quarter are obese. Nearly a third (31 per cent) of UK children aged 2–15 years are overweight or obese. According to the World Health Organization (WHO), 74 per cent of UK men and 64 per cent of UK women will be overweight by 2030. Around the world, too, these estimates have been steadily rising and researchers say there is no evidence that most countries have even reached a plateau in obesity levels, let alone resolved the problem.

The clearest culprit for the global weight crisis is our obesogenic society, with opportunities for overconsumption everywhere, the normalizing of constant snacking and more cheap energy-dense food and 2-for-1 supermarket offers than ever before. At the same time, our environment also discourages physical activity. Compared with two or three decades ago, when children played on their bikes or in the park or ran around outdoors, nowadays most children stay home indoors, playing computer games or interacting online. The same is true for adults: less walking to the shop or the office, more online convenience and sedentary work or driving in cars.

Whatever the rights and wrongs of modern society, there is no doubt that becoming overweight or obese carries genuine health risks. Conditions associated with excess weight include coronary heart disease, angina and stroke, diabetes, hypertension, arthritis, cataracts, liver and kidney disease, respiratory and sleep problems and infertility, to name but a few. In 2016, the WHO reported that excess fat causes twice as many cancers as previously thought, including cancers of the liver, stomach, bone marrow and ovary. Predicting a 'world epidemic', WHO scientists have also linked obesity to cancers of the gallbladder, pancreas, thyroid, brain and prostate. This makes obesity the biggest single preventable cause of cancer after smoking.

As well as the serious physical risks, being overweight also causes emotional distress, ranging from depression and loneliness to more serious mental illnesses.

OBSESSIVE COMPULSIVE DISORDER (OCD)

OCD is classified as an anxiety disorder. It is estimated that OCD affects around 12 in every 1000 people in the UK, or 1.2 per cent of the population, across the age, gender, racial and socioeconomic range. The WHO ranks OCD in the top ten most disabling illnesses, as measured in terms of lost earnings and diminished quality of life.

An individual with OCD feels compelled to carry out repetitive rituals in order to try to counter or neutralize intrusive thoughts. These thoughts are usually recurrent, and the rituals and thoughts tend to escalate. For example, checking a few times a day that the oven is turned off might become an hourly habit. The more that the ritual fails to provide reassurance or relief, the more the action is repeated. In 1875, the French psychiatrist Legrand du Saulle described OCD as the 'folie du doute' – the doubting disease. Individuals constantly doubt themselves and are locked into a cycle of repeating a ritual in order to reassure themselves that things will be OK. They often recognize that their OCD behaviours are not rational, but are nonetheless unable to break out of the cycle.

Common OCD rituals include excessive cleaning or washing, repeatedly seeking reassurance from others, constantly checking locks on doors, checking that light switches, taps or cookers are turned off, and hoarding. Individuals with OCD may avoid certain numbers, they may fear contamination or attach undue significance to normal daily events. Many of these actions are not problematic in themselves: cleaning, locking doors and switching off ovens are important everyday habits. Checking once (or twice) that the car door is locked is perfectly normal. The problem arises when the actions become 'obsessive' and 'compulsive', and prevent a person from functioning adequately in daily life.

Individuals with OCD tend to ruminate; they get trapped in a cycle and are unable to 'change the record', as it were. Although we all have a tendency to dwell on things, in severe cases of OCD thoughts and images may be deeply disturbing, involving harm to oneself or loved ones or fear of catastrophic consequences that will arise if the compulsive ritual is not performed. Individuals may feel guilty or full of dread or they may imagine committing violent acts – although it is very rare for them to actually carry these out.

The checking or cleaning ritual itself may have no connection with the disturbing thoughts: compulsive hand-washing may have little to do with concerns about hygiene, and no connection with the persistent and disturbing thoughts. Somehow though, the compulsion provides temporary relief until the persistent thoughts recur, thereby reinforcing the cycle of OCD.

OCD can interfere with every area of a person's life, including school, work, family and personal relationships. While we all worry about loved ones falling ill or getting hurt, and we all have habits, preferences and superstitions, these are usually enjoyable, comforting or just a part of our daily routine. In order to be diagnosed with OCD, an individual's patterns of behaviour must be considered to cause significant impairment, distress and anxiety, and be time-consuming.

The neurotransmitter serotonin (see **SEROTONIN**) plays a key role in how the brain checks for errors and omissions. Low levels of carbohydrate affect levels of serotonin, which can exacerbate symptoms of OCD. Individuals with anorexia usually limit their carbohydrate intake and commonly experience obsessive, anxiety-driven behaviours. When nutritional balance and carbohydrate intake are restored, these checking and anxiety-focused behaviours decrease or disappear completely

CBT is a highly effective treatment for combatting OCD. A trained therapist will guide the individual to challenge their intrusive thoughts giving them the confidence to reduce, and eventually cease, the problematic repetitive rituals.

OEDEMA

Water retention, or oedema, is a common side effect of disordered eating behaviour. Purging through laxative and diuretic abuse or vomiting, or restrictive dieting, often leads to extreme dehydration and 'rebound' water retention. Water retention is worst after stopping laxatives or after vomiting, when the body can hold on to as much as 4 or 5 kg of 'water weight'. Malnutrition, insufficient protein or bingeing on salty foods will further exacerbate this.

Anorexic individuals may also experience oedema when they restart normal eating after prolonged starving. This is known as refeeding oedema and is not an increase in actual body weight, but it can be highly distressing for individuals who are already anxious about their shape and size. Instead of allowing the body to rebalance, to rehydrate and to lose the excess fluid, the person often panics, triggering the vicious cycle of trying to lose weight and emptying the body all over again. It is important to understand that oedema is a natural reaction to starving or purging. Given adequate nutrition and a chance to recover, the body will rebalance itself and lose the excess fluid, and with it the water weight. Reassurance and continued nourishment are essential during the refeeding (and weight restoration) process. Oedema is not sudden weight gain and will resolve as the body rehydrates and heals.

ORTHOREXIA

The term 'orthorexia', meaning correct diet, was coined in 1997 by Dr Steven Bratman to describe an unhealthy fixation with healthy eating. In recent years, orthorexia has become recognized as an increasingly widespread condition that causes real health problems. Orthorexia is not officially recognized by the American Psychiatric

Association as an eating disorder, and is not listed in the latest (5th) edition of the DSM. However, many specialists believe that orthorexia is an eating disorder in disguise – more socially respectable, but no less restrictive.

Orthorexia resembles other eating disorders in the rigidity and guilt of the mindset: while anorexics or bulimics obsess about calories and weight, orthorexics obsess about the purity of their diet. Orthorexia overlaps with anorexia and other eating disorders, and is increasingly mainstream, somewhere on the blurred boundary between being normally health-conscious and abnormally health-obsessed. Orthorexia is defined as a 'fixation with righteous or correct eating' – but what begins as an attempt to improve one's lifestyle can morph into an unhealthy fixation with the 'perfect' diet. It can lead to self-loathing, low self-esteem, social isolation and even malnourishment.

Orthorexia thrives in a society obsessed with 'wellness' in which we are urged to lose weight, count calories, avoid artificial additives and preservatives, and beware plastic packaging and hidden toxins (see also **CLEAN EATING**). Individuals with severe orthorexia may find their social interactions limited by their need for 'pure' and natural food. Relationships and family life may be hindered by intrusive obsessions with healthy eating, and sleep, mood, work and health may suffer. The more rigid their self-imposed rules, the more lonely and preoccupied with 'wellness' they become.

As in clean eating, the orthorexic mindset revolves around vague and unscientific notions of so-called toxins and chemicals. It focuses on purity and the need to cleanse and detoxify the body from inside. Even the occasional 'bad' food, sweet treat or processed substance will induce guilt, which makes eating out with friends very difficult. On top of these rigid eating rules, many orthorexics also display signs of exercise addiction: needing to work out every single day, exercising despite illness or injury or showing distress when they are not able to go to the gym. The pressure to look good, train hard and restrict calories is intense, especially among young women. Instagram (see **SOCIAL MEDIA**) is awash with post-workout selfies, along with the obligatory green juice or protein shake (instead of food). Sales of athleisure wear – stylish and expensive workout gear – are at an all-time high; hashtags such as #go hard or go home reinforce the message.

While this is not a problem for most people, it is extremely unhelpful for those who are predisposed to disordered eating and exercise addiction or are already unwell. Society's widespread approval of self-discipline and self-denial for them turns into self-destructive behaviour. Paradoxically, social approval of 'healthy' lifestyles means that those with orthorexia, for example, come to feel validated in their obsession with clean eating and exercise. This fuels their damaging orthorexic habits, and can lead to the development of anorexia or bulimia nervosa.

Those with orthorexic and anorexic tendencies are particularly vulnerable to persuasion, or even misinformation, around nutrition and wellness. Unscientific lifestyle messages about the evils of dairy or grains, for example, seem to hit home most effectively in those already prone to disordered eating.

OSTEOPOROSIS/OSTEOPENIA

It's a sad and shocking fact that up to 90 per cent of individuals with anorexia show some degree of bone loss. After the age of 30 years, the average woman loses around 1 per cent of bone density a year. All women are at risk of thinning bones as they age, especially after the menopause, when levels of oestrogen decline rapidly, but this risk is particularly severe in females with anorexia. Unfortunately, they fulfil all the criteria for bone depletion: amenorrhoea (loss of periods), which leads to lack of oestrogen, too low body weight and an inadequate intake of calcium (see **CALCIUM**). They may also be taking excessive exercise, which can further weaken the bones. Additionally, anorexic and restrictive behaviour usually occurs during the most crucial phase of women's lives: in their teens and twenties, young women need to lay down bone mass as protection against natural bone thinning in later life.

Osteopenia is the precursor to full-blown osteoporosis. The condition is measured by dual-emission X-ray absorptiometry (DEXA), a technique that measures bone mineral density. Bone thinning is serious, but to some extent reversible: with restoration of body weight and menstrual periods, bone mass can recover, although of course this is dependent on age (the earlier the reversal, the better). The damage of osteopenia and osteoporosis is invisible at first, but nonetheless young women should be aware of the possible consequences in later life: not only an elevated risk of fractures, weak and brittle bones, but also a loss of height due to a crumbling spine. The sooner anorexia is treated and weight is restored, the better the chance of avoiding osteoporosis.

OVEREATING

See **BINGE-EATING DISORDER**.

P

PARAESTHESIA

This refers to abnormal tingling or prickling sensations, commonly in the hands or feet. Paraesthesia, numbness and muscles spasms in eating disorders may be a sign of dietary deficiencies and general malnutrition.

PATHOREXIA

Pathorexia refers to disordered appetite and the whole spectrum of eating disorders.

PEER PRESSURE

Although friends can be an important source of support for someone with an eating disorder, they can also be a cause for concern. It is well known that disordered eating and excessive body-image anxiety thrive in high-pressure environments, often female and often academic, such as girls' private schools and universities.

Peer pressure is a risk that presents during childhood and adolescence, when we are particularly vulnerable to the influence of others in our age group. We worry about what they think of us, are keen to be part of the gang and 'join in' with whatever they are doing. This could be underage drinking, smoking or other risky behaviours. Unfortunately, in the case of teenage girls, it's often competitive weight loss through restricting and purging. The pressure from peers to be thin and cool, to skip meals and to exercise, is compounded by the pressures from social media to show off the perfect body and the perfect life.

PERFECTIONISM

There is nothing wrong with being ambitious and wanting to do your best. Perfectionism can be a positive character trait, within reason. However, striving for perfection all the time leads to anxiety, dissatisfaction and low self-esteem. And when taken to extremes, perfectionism risks becoming dangerous, even self-destructive.

Unhealthy perfectionism is common among individuals with eating disorders, especially those with anorexia. The positive 'perfectionist' drive, to perform well in exams or at work, to eat healthily, to look good, morphs into a negative cycle of unrealistic targets and constant self-criticism. The anorexic perfectionist monologue focuses on food and appearance, but also affects other areas of life: 'Whatever I achieve, it will never be good enough', 'I wish I had more self-discipline and could restrict food/exercise more', 'I'll never get the perfect body', 'No matter how hard I try, I'll never look as good as those girls.'

Of course, these thoughts are normal for most adolescents, but the danger starts when perfectionism gets out of control. The anorexic voice itself is never satisfied: calorie intake can always be reduced, intense exercise can always be increased.

The most important step when tackling perfectionism is to stop and take a reality check. Making comparisons with others (friends, strangers, supermodels) is futile and guaranteed to bring you down. As we know (see **SOCIAL MEDIA**), everyone posts their highlights reel online, not the real thing. We all edit and beautify the good bits of our lives, and leave out the boring or ugly bits. Comparing yourself with airbrushed images of models is simply pointless: they have a dedicated team of make-up artists, stylists, dietitians and personal trainers; you do not. Take time every day to disconnect from social media and, if possible, take digital detox weekends.

The next step is challenging the self-critical monologue, ideally with a CBT therapist (see **COGNITIVE BEHAVIOURAL THERAPY**) or within a group setting.

Relaxation exercises are also very effective at stilling the perfectionist tendency to obsess, compare and despair. This could be meditation, deep breathing or just going for a walk in nature. Turn off your phone and disconnect from the virtual world, celebrity websites and social media. Get involved in something real, volunteer to help others, write a short story, anything that distracts you from the anxious worrying.

Finally, break some rules. Perfectionists, especially those with anorexia, live by a rigid and exhausting set of self-imposed rules. Eat something from your list of 'unsafe' foods; ignore your alarm and have a lie-in; skip your daily workout. If that's too radical, start small: can you leave your bed unmade, just for one day?

Perfectionism in anorexia comes from fear of change, fear of the unexpected and a desperate need for control, but it ends up taking over your life. Each time you challenge your rigid perfectionist rules, you are one step closer to regaining control, choice and freedom.

PERIODS

See **AMENORRHOEA**.

PERSONALITY/PERSONALITY TRAITS

Specific personality traits have been consistently associated with eating disorders and are therefore thought to be risk factors. In anorexia and bulimia, people display high levels of perfectionism, setting and pursuing unrealistically high standards for themselves. They display obsessive or compulsive habits, constantly doubting, checking and needing order and control. Anorexia and bulimia are characterized by neuroticism, harm avoidance, low cooperativeness and other avoidant personality traits. Individuals also show narcissism, sociotropy (concern with acceptance and approval from others) and autonomy (seeking independence, control and achievement).

In BED and bulimia, typical traits include high impulsivity, often defined as a lack of forethought or a failure to contemplate the consequences before acting. Other BED and bulimia traits include sensation-seeking and novelty-seeking, and a readiness to take physical or social risks in order to seek out new experiences.

Of course, many of these personality traits are also seen in those who do *not* have eating disorders, but they are found consistently and more markedly among individuals with an eating disorder than among control groups. The question is whether these personality traits are causal or a consequence of the eating disorder. Are they risk factors or an outcome? We know that extreme food restriction and other disordered eating behaviours affect many aspects of the body's complex neurochemical, biological and cognitive processes. Traits such as obsessionality and rigidity may be a direct result of semi-starvation or exacerbated by it. Some individuals continue to display these traits after recovery, whereas others show improved symptoms and reduced personality difficulties.

Maintaining a serious eating disorder is exhausting and distressing, and it really does change your normal personality. Someone who is naturally open and friendly may become withdrawn or secretive. Someone who loves socializing may avoid others in order to pursue their bingeing behaviour in private. They may lie about what they have eaten or steal to buy food. They may become secretive, dishonest or irritable. Starving alters the brain chemistry and makes people depressed, listless, even aggressive. Think of how normal people get 'tetchy' when they are hungry; anorexia is a magnified version of this constant hunger. Constantly bingeing or purging has similar negative effects on the mind and the body.

Sudden mood swings are also common, with rapid shifts from depression to elation, despair to anger. Individuals may become obsessive about food, eating rituals, timing of meals or cooking for others (see also **OBSESSIVE COMPULSIVE DISORDER**).

All these mood changes, as well as the behavioural and medical issues, are very hard for those close to the person to understand. Family, partners and friends may feel pushed away when they are trying to help; they may not recognize the person they love. The person may not even recognize him- or herself. It is important to understand that these personality changes are not part of the individuals themselves, nor are they permanent; they are due to the physiological imbalances created by disordered eating.

PERSONALITY/PERSONALITY TRAITS

Talking therapies and medication will help to stabilize the condition, but the most important thing is regular, balanced nutrition and a restoration of healthy body weight. Negative psychological changes should reverse once the individual is on the road to physical recovery.

Personality changes sometimes appear to be more serious. In such cases, professional advice should be sought. Risk-taking and impulsivity are known side effects of eating disorders, so if an individual reports self-harming or has suicidal thoughts or plans, you should seek medical help.

PERSONALITY DISORDERS

Some of the personality disorders linked with eating disorders include dependent personality disorder, borderline personality disorder and obsessive compulsive personality disorder (OCPD). (Note that OCPD is different from OCD – the first is a personality disorder and the second is an anxiety disorder. Although some individuals with OCPD do have OCD, they are considered to be distinct disorders.) Any of these personality disorders may pre-date the onset of the eating disorder or they may have developed alongside the illness. In all cases, professional psychiatric care is advised for the management of these conditions.

PORTION SIZE

How much we eat is as important as what we eat. Undereaters and overeaters often lose a sense of what's 'normal' (see **NORMAL DIET**) and get locked into very restrictive or excessive eating patterns. The more irregular and secretive their behaviour becomes, the harder it is for them to visualize what the average person might eat. For this reason, judgement and insight can become skewed in individuals with eating disorders. For example, those with anorexia routinely overestimate their own body size and, at the other end of the spectrum, binge-eaters are often horrified at the realization that they have eaten thousands of calories in a single episode.

There are physical implications too: when your stomach is accustomed to extremely tiny or very large amounts of food, it is uncomfortable to eat more or less. A binge-eater will struggle to feel full on a regular-sized portion, and an anorexic will struggle to finish it all. Bulimic individuals may also struggle with the feeling of fullness if they are accustomed to emptying their stomach by purging after eating. This is all part of the process of recovery, like buying clothes in larger sizes or not vomiting after meals or starting to eat in public with others. There may also be 'unsafe' or fear foods, such as fat, or foods that trigger a loss of control, such as carbohydrates.

In a practical sense, portion control is a good place to start. Although 'normal' doesn't really exist – for example, the USA is known for its much bigger restaurant meals – there are nevertheless broad norms for how much an individual should eat at an average mealtime. Increasing or decreasing portion sizes can help with gaining or losing weight in a healthy way. Recovering from an eating disorder takes time, perseverance and patience, and keeping a good perspective on normal eating can really help.

POTASSIUM

Potassium is a mineral that plays a vital role in the human body. As a chemical partner of sodium, potassium helps to move water around the body as required. It enables nutrients to move into, and waste to move out of, cells. It is used to keep fluids in balance inside all cells, particularly the brain cells. Potassium is also essential for healthy nerve and muscle functioning, and for the secretion of insulin for blood sugar control.

Eating-disordered behaviours, especially vomiting and other forms of purging, disrupt potassium levels, causing hypokalaemia – low blood potassium levels. These low levels cause fatigue, drowsiness, muscle weakness and, in serious cases, cardiac arrhythmia, muscle paralysis and even death (see **BULIMIA NERVOSA**, **ELECTROLYTES** and **VOMITING**). Dietary sources of potassium include whole grains, lean meat, green leafy vegetables, mushrooms and beans.

PSYCHONUTRITION

See **NORADRENALINE, SEROTONIN, ANXIETY** and **OBSES-SIVE COMPULSIVE DISORDER.**

PURGING

This refers to both vomiting and use of laxatives. Repeated bingeing and purging, as in bulimia, has serious consequences for the body's digestive process and overall health. (See also **VOMITING** and **LAXATIVES.**)

q

QUINOA

It's been cultivated for thousands of years in South America, but quinoa has only attained superfood status in the West in the past few years (see also **SUPERFOODS**). Known to Inca tribes as 'the mother of all grains' and considered to be a sacred crop, quinoa was even celebrated by the United Nations, which dubbed 2013 'The International Year of Quinoa'.

Although it's widely thought of as a grain, quinoa is botanically classified as a non-grassy plant or pseudo-cereal, closely related to beetroot, spinach, and amaranth. Nutritionally, however, quinoa is considered to be a whole grain because it contains its entire grain seed intact (unlike processed or refined white bread, pasta or flour).

Whether or not you buy into the marketing hype, there's no doubt that quinoa is highly nutritious and bursting with protein. It's one of the few plant foods to contain all nine essential amino acids. Quinoa is therefore an excellent plant-based protein source for vegetarians and vegans.

For those with coeliac disease or who are allergic to or have an intolerance of gluten, quinoa is naturally gluten-free and high in fibre, so is considered much healthier than artificial gluten-free foods, most of which contain corn, rice or potato flour and other refined starches.

Quinoa is high in magnesium, the B vitamins, iron, potassium, calcium, phosphorus, vitamin E and various important antioxidants. Countless studies have linked the consumption of quinoa (and other whole grains) to lower levels of cardiovascular disease, type 2 diabetes, high blood pressure, colon cancer and obesity. Quinoa also contains beneficial fatty acids.

There are hundreds of cultivated types of quinoa, but the ones most commonly available in our shops are the white, red and black grains. Quinoa is used in a wide range of recipes, from sweet to savoury, such as porridge, brownies and crunchy breakfast bars, as well as salads, chilli, stir-fries and burgers.

r

RECOVERY

Overcoming an eating disorder is a process of physical *and* mental recovery, and both aspects are crucial. One without the other is likely to have limited success. During recovery, you will have to face emotional, psychological and practical issues, tackling how you feel about food, about your body, about who you are and what you deserve. Recovery, especially in anorexia, focuses on restoration of weight, but it involves many other things too. You will need to face up to some difficult truths about your own behaviour and possible causes. Lasting recovery is hard work and takes a willingness to be honest with yourself and others. Above all, it takes perseverance, determination and grit.

In terms of physical recovery, the rate of healing may be much slower than the rate at which damage occurs: for example, the bone loss that occurs over two to three years in anorexia may take eight to ten years to reverse. Similarly, although the weight loss may have been relatively rapid, it may take months or years to return to a stable, healthy weight. Amenorrhoea may also take a long time to reverse: recovering anorexics often find that the weight at which menses return is higher than the weight at which they stopped. This can be frustrating and confusing. Some physical changes, such as the damage done to tooth enamel by repeated vomiting, are not reversible.

In severe eating disorders, recovery rates are low and relapse rates are high. While some people only experience an eating disorder for a few months, others may be ill for many years and never overcome it.

So is it ever possible to recover fully from a severe eating disorder? Admittedly, there is no silver bullet and recovery may not be a linear process: some days it will feel like one step forward and two steps back. It is also important to remember that recovery will not solve everything. When your eating becomes less disordered, many things will improve – but life may still be full of difficulties and challenges, as it is for most people. Recovery means making the decision that starving, purging or bingeing is not going to be your escape route.

Recovery can also be a painful process. You may have been ill or in hospital for many years, you may have isolated yourself, hated your body, cut yourself off from friends. Even once you regain physical health, it will take time to heal mentally and emotionally (see also **SELF-COMPASSION**).

With a good support network and a strong personal reason to recover (see **MOTIVATION**), you can keep going despite the setbacks. Talk to others who have recovered fully and you will see that it's worth the effort.

REFEEDING

There are different methods of refeeding depending on the severity of the eating disorder (see also **WEIGHT GAIN**).

Individuals with anorexia nervosa who understand that they need to gain weight may attend an eating disorders clinic on an outpatient basis. Working with their therapist and dietitian, they can follow an agreed meal plan, attend group sessions and participate in other occupational therapies. The calorie and nutritional composition of their meals will be monitored and they will be supported during and after mealtimes if they experience distress.

In more severe cases, where an individual is dangerously underweight and unwilling or unable to contemplate weight gain, hospitalization is required. Depending on the individual's physical condition, hospital refeeding may take the form of intravenous feeding, nasogastric intubation or a combination of the two.

RELAPSE

See **LAPSES** and **RECOVERY**.

RELATIONSHIPS

See **FAMILY**, **FRIENDS** and **SEX**.

REST

Ask any athlete or personal trainer and they will tell you that regular rest is as important as regular exercise. A strong, healthy body needs time to recover in between bouts of activity. This doesn't mean switching to a different exercise or doing slightly less; this means whole days where you do not exercise vigorously. Before running the four-minute mile in 1954, Sir Roger Bannister did not run for five days. He gave his body total rest, and on race day his legs were fresh, his energy levels were high and he broke the world record.

RITUALS

See **OBSESSIVE COMPULSIVE DISORDER**.

ROLE MODELS

In the field of eating disorders, these are traditionally considered to be a Bad Thing. Role models are often female models or actresses who are seen as promoting an unhealthily thin body ideal to vulnerable young women. Whether or not these role models really cause mental illness is debatable, but we can all agree that unrealistic airbrushed media images can be unhelpful to those who are unhappy with their weight or insecure about their bodies.

However, there is a much healthier side to role models: real people who can guide you in recovery, not faceless celebrities. Look around you at the people you admire; how do they eat? In your own life, this might be a sister or a friend, a teacher or a colleague. There are so many people out there who genuinely love their food, eat with gusto, don't bother with diets and maintain a stable, healthy weight! You may be able to confide in them or you may prefer to observe from afar. Watch how naturally they respond to their body's appetite: they don't ignore their hunger pangs or squirrel food away to eat in secret. They don't care what other people are eating, and they don't express guilt after meals. Finding a role model like this can be a wonderful example in your own recovery. If they can eat regularly and healthily, with occasional treats, without punishing themselves at the gym, and without starving or bingeing, so can you.

RUNNING

See **EXERCISE**.

S

SCALES

Body weight is one of the central preoccupations of individuals with eating disorders, and stepping on the bathroom scales becomes an obsession. Minor fluctuations in weight set off a cycle of yet more restrictive dieting, over-exercising and purging behaviours in those with anorexia and bulimia. Not only do their weight fluctuations plunge them into despair but they also cannot believe it is possible. It takes around 3,500 calories to gain 1 pound of body fat – so how can they have gained several pounds in weight when they're barely eating anything?

The truth is, minor fluctuations in weight are perfectly normal. Most human beings, weighed morning and evening, will show an average weight difference of between 2 and 4 pounds. There are many physiological reasons why scale weight fluctuates, none of them to do with actual body weight. Women in particular see marked fluctuations of weight during their menstrual cycle, usually in the week before and during their period. Fluctuating hormones can account for as much as 5 pounds, but this is water weight, not body fat.

Alcohol is another reason for weight fluctuation: it acts as a diuretic, causing dehydration, which leads to water retention. The water retention is a result of your body wanting to make up for the difference in water levels that drinking alcohol has caused. Other causes of dehydration include illness and hot weather, and these can cause a drop in the figure on the scales.

Weight will also fluctuate before and after emptying the bladder and bowel, with a difference of around 1 to 3 pounds.

Sodium also contributes to water retention, with an increased intake of salty food causing your body to retain more water. Bingeing on carbohydrates contributes to water retention, as they affect glycogen stores and fluid balance. Some strength training also results in weight fluctuation, as muscles retain water in cells as part of healing and laying down new muscle fibres.

As well as these normal fluctuations, individuals with bulimia may be relying on the use of laxatives and diuretics. As we have seen, this interferes with the natural fluid balance and gives a skewed body weight.

The moral of the story is: don't become a slave to your bathroom scales. Too many women (even those without eating disorders) start the morning by weighing themselves; surveys have shown that their entire day can be ruined by feeling 'fat'. This dependence on the scales is illogical and arbitrary: the number on the scales is not written on your forehead for all to see. Bathroom scales are useful for assessing the general direction of weight gain or loss in the long term, but they are inaccurate and unhelpful if used on a daily basis. Individuals with anorexia are the most vulnerable and should only be weighed in a clinical setting with their therapist there to discuss feelings about weight gain or loss.

Remember, weighing yourself numerous times a day is unnecessary and unhealthy. Instead of scales, use your logic. Did you eat ten thousand calories yesterday? Of course not. Do your clothes feel radically tighter than yesterday? Of course not. Remember that weight gain takes months of overeating; it doesn't happen magically overnight. During the sensitive period of refeeding and restoring a healthy body weight, the bathroom scales are really not your friend. You are a flesh-and-blood human being, not a sack of flour.

SELECTIVE SEROTONIN REUPTAKE INHIBITORS (SSRIs)

This group of drugs is mainly used to treat depression. They are also used in eating disorders, OCD and other anxiety and panic disorders. The most widely used SSRIs are fluoxetine (also known as

Prozac) and sertraline, both medications frequently used for individuals with eating disorders.

SSRIs work by blocking the reabsorption of the neurotransmitter serotonin (see **SEROTONIN**) following its release in the brain. This non-absorption leads to increased serotonin levels and an improvement in mood. SSRIs have been shown to have fewer side effects than older antidepressant drugs (tricylic antidepressants and MAOIs) and are less dangerous in overdose, although they may cause nausea, anxiety or restlessness. SSRIs are generally not prescribed for those under 18 years of age.

SELENIUM

The trace element selenium is necessary for many biological processes within the body. It reduces inflammation, strengthens the immune system to fight infection, supports a healthy heart, reproductive system and metabolism, and helps to preserve the elasticity of body tissues. Selenium has antioxidant properties that help to protect against free radicals and carcinogens. Good food sources include meat, fish, whole grains and dairy products.

SELF-COMPASSION

Most individuals with disordered eating have been disliking, even harming themselves, for years. Deciding to like yourself again, learning how to listen to and care for your body's needs, are crucial in the recovery process.

Kindness to oneself is as important as kindness to others. It is shocking to realize just how unkind we can be to ourselves, whether mentally or physically. Automatic negative thoughts are common in many of us (see **COGNITIVE BEHAVIOURAL THERAPY** and **LANGUAGE**). Many women habitually tell themselves they're fat or unattractive, that they don't deserve to be in a good relationship or to get a promotion. They are continually trying to eat less, lose weight and always comparing themselves with others. It's no wonder that many women feel dissatisfied or angry with their bodies. Individuals with eating disorders routinely report disliking their personalities too: how they *are* as well as how they *look*.

Spend a few hours tuning in to your inner monologue. What unkind things are you saying? Could you imagine saying them to a friend? Can you catch these inner negative thoughts as they arise, and question them? Could you even give yourself some compliments?

Learning self-compassion is hard but essential. When you respect yourself, you begin to understand what you really need. Thirst, hunger, sadness and boredom are all very different needs. Sometimes you need food, but sometimes you need a hug or a chat or a rest. Being kind to yourself naturally helps to reduce self-harming behaviours such as starving and purging: when you truly value your body, you don't want to harm it.

SELF-HARM

Also referred to as non-suicidal self-injury, this refers to deliberately injuring, hurting or putting oneself at risk. Sadly, up to 72 per cent of people with an eating disorder have also engaged in non-suicidal self-injury or self-harm.

Self-harm usually takes the form of physical mutilation, such as cutting the arm or leg or burning oneself with cigarettes. Self-harm most often occurs among young people, and is three times more common among women than men. It often arises as a response to childhood abuse or during periods of intense emotional distress. Individuals who self-harm report that hurting themselves physically gives them temporary relief from their mental turmoil: the act of injuring is a kind of release. Some people say they feel numb or dead inside, others harm as a way of punishing themselves or to regain control. The individual may self-harm only occasionally, at times of crisis, or it may become a regular habit. Individuals may hide their injuries – for example, wearing long sleeves even in hot weather – or they may flaunt them.

Self-harm covers a wide range of behaviours. It does not always take the form of a physical injury. In the context of eating disorders, anorexia, bulimia and binge-eating are also forms of self-harm. Starving oneself, bingeing on large amounts of food, self-induced vomiting and overdosing on laxatives are all harmful to the body. Self-harm can also take the form of personal neglect, where individuals fail to meet their basic needs, such as washing, staying warm, staying safe.

CBT, relaxation exercises and anger management techniques can help to reduce the frequency and intensity of self-harming behaviours. All self-injury is potentially dangerous, and professional advice should always be sought.

SEROTONIN

Serotonin is an important chemical neurotransmitter in the brain. One of its key functions is the regulation of mood and emotional states such as depression, aggression and irritability. Serotonin is also involved in a range of other physiological processes, including bowel function, bone density, blood clotting, nausea and sexual function. Serotonin is manufactured in the brain and the intestines, with around 80 to 90 per cent of the body's serotonin found in the gastrointestinal tract.

Although food cannot directly increase the serotonin supply, nonetheless nutrition plays an important role in serotonin levels and mood balancing: many nutrients increase levels of tryptophan, the amino acid from which serotonin is made. Carbohydrates play an essential part in the release of insulin, which increases uptake of serotonin in the brain: tryptophan remains in the bloodstream at high levels following a carbohydrate-rich meal, which means it can freely enter the brain and cause serotonin levels to rise. When carbs are restricted, as in anorexia, serotonin levels become depleted. This may also explain why individuals with anorexia who avoid carbo-hydrates may experience depression, mood swings, irritability and checking behaviours (the kind common in OCD). Serotonin also induces and maintains sleep, including sleep.

In severe malnutrition, SSRI antidepressants, such as Prozac, cannot work effectively, since there is no serotonin for them to act upon.

SET POINT THEORY

Set point theory suggests that our body weight is automatically regulated to remain within a certain range, like an inner thermostat. The set point is the level at which the body functions optimally. Set point theory argues that the body will fight to remain at or around its natural set point, usually a range of from 10 to 20 pounds, within which you will be comfortable and function well. Just as we have different eye and hair colours, so we all have a different set point. This is determined by our individual biology and genetics, not by diet or exercise. This theory explains why some people are naturally thinner or fatter than others and some people are able to eat a lot without gaining weight, whereas others gain weight easily and struggle to lose weight and keep it off.

Set point theory is enlightening to anyone with an eating disorder or those constantly battling their own appetite to try to lose weight. Learning to accept the fact that your body needs to be at a certain weight is a good way to stop the vicious cycle of dieting and disordered eating. Drastically restricting your food intake simply slows down your metabolism, as your body tries to adjust to fewer calories. The more you try to go below your natural set point range, the harder your body will strive to retain its natural weight.

SEX

Along with food, sex is one of the most fundamental and instinctive of all human appetites. It is clear that malnutrition and low BMI have a significant impact on libido. Severe anorexia and restrictive/purging behaviours affect all the body's physiological functions, including sex drive. Low body weight and poor nutrition have a direct impact on the production of sex hormones. Fat is necessary for the production of oestrogen, a vital sex hormone in women. The ovaries, which are also the source of 50 per cent of testosterone in women, become less active, decreasing the production of the sex hormones that are key to female libido. As oestrogen and testosterone both decline, sex drive is reduced.

Low body weight not only disrupts the body's hormonal balance but also has a major emotional and psychological impact. When someone feels negatively towards their own body, it can be challenging to establish physical intimacy with a partner. The central features of eating disorders such as distorted body image, body dissatisfaction and shame can compromise healthy sexual functioning and relationships. Self-acceptance of one's own body is fundamental to being intimate with someone else. Romantic relationships require trust, and sexual pleasure requires a degree of physical abandonment. Eating disorders are all about control, so it can be very hard to trust or let go.

Women with anorexia report greater loss of libido than those with bulimia and other eating disorders. Studies have found that the lower the BMI, the greater the sexual anxiety, loss of desire and avoidance of intimate relationships. Clearly, when the body is severely malnourished, as in anorexia, sex is not the first priority.

Men with anorexia also experience sexual dysfunction and problems with fertility due to low levels of testosterone.

Libido in both women and men is usually restored in line with weight restoration and general physical recovery, but psychological recovery may take longer. In cases where sexual abuse or trauma underlie the eating disorder, professional support is essential.

SHAME

All eating disorders involve a significant degree of shame. Because the person's behaviour around food has become so dysfunctional, the act of eating itself feels shameful. Most anorexics and binge-eaters will avoid (and fear) eating in public. In anorexia, individuals worry about their unusual habits: cutting food into small pieces, making a tiny portion last a long time, worrying about how they chew, how they sit, whether they 'look greedy'. In BED, individuals who are overweight report feeling judged on their food choices, the amount they eat and of course their size. They often experience discomfort and shame when shopping in supermarkets or having lunch in a café.

These are complicated feelings, and they go some way to explaining why the individual ends up hiding away and eating in private. The more secretive eating becomes, the harder it becomes to eat in public. Unfortunately, the sense of scrutiny is not just imagined: the general public do stare when they see a severely underweight or overweight person, and they may well be curious to see them eating.

CBT for eating disorders often involves eating in public, sometimes with the therapist or a friend, to address these emotions of shame around food. It's an important part of challenging disordered patterns and re-establishing eating as a normal part of daily life.

Shame goes far wider than food and eating, of course. Many overweight individuals feel intense shame about their bodies. They may have been teased from childhood for being 'fat', and may have struggled to lose weight all their life. Changing rooms, swimming pools and beach holidays are fraught with anxiety due to these individuals' weight and body shape. Shame is a powerful emotion, but it can be overcome.

Anorexics also feel shame about their bodies: it's a myth that all anorexics think they are fat. Many underweight individuals are aware of the physical ravages of their illness. They feel ashamed and disgusted at how emaciated they have become, but powerless to gain weight.

SLEEP

Disordered eating tends to lead to disrupted sleep. Being overweight is a common cause of sleep disorders, including sleep apnoea. Obstructive sleep apnoea causes snoring and temporary obstruction of the air flow, which can be dangerous. In serious cases, obstructive sleep apnoea may lead to accidents due to tiredness in the daytime, as well as risks of stroke or heart attack at night. The condition is often aggravated by alcohol and sleeping pills.

Being underweight also makes sleeping physically difficult. Someone who is very thin lacks the natural padding around their bones, making it painful to lie in one position for a long time, even on a soft mattress.

Hunger is a major cause of insomnia: if the body needs food, it will remain awake and anxious, unable to power down. Just as a baby cries when it's hungry, so our bodies cannot switch off and drift into sleep when they have not been fed.

Being too hungry is bad for sleep, but so is being too full. Binges or overeating episodes often take place at night, leaving the body struggling to digest a large amount of food. In BED, sleep may be disrupted by night-time eating, as this is the only opportunity for privacy (see **NIGHT-EATING SYNDROME**).

As suggested by the saying 'breakfast like a king, lunch like a prince and dine like a pauper', daytime is in general more conducive to digestion than night-time is. The body is naturally active and moving around during the day, and therefore able to use the energy, as well as carrying out all the other digestive processes smoothly. Most dietitians recommend eating your evening meal at least two hours before bedtime.

Anxiety is a central feature of most eating disorders and it interferes with sleep. People with anorexia or orthorexia lie awake at night obsessively counting up the calories they have consumed or planning what they will eat the next day.

Whatever the causes, prolonged sleep deprivation has a negative impact. Individuals may experience irritability, poor memory, short attention for work or study, depression and even paranoia. In the majority of cases, sleep improves as eating patterns improve, and as a healthy body weight is restored. (For foods that help to promote sleep, see **MELATONIN**.)

SLEEP HYGIENE

As outlined above, a regular, balanced diet is essential for good quality sleep. As well as eating well for sleep (see **MELATONIN**), there are other eating and drinking habits to avoid. Two important substances to avoid are caffeine and alcohol.

Caffeine is a stimulant found in many foods and drinks – not just coffee – that stays in your system for hours (caffeine has a half-life of up to seven hours). If you are prone to insomnia, limit your caffeine consumption to the morning or switch to decaffeinated versions. You could see a marked difference in your quality of sleep. Don't forget that chocolate, tea and many soft drinks also contain caffeine. Green tea is a good alternative: it contains around 25 mg of caffeine, compared with 150 mg in a latte.

Avoid drinking excessive amounts of alcohol, especially right before bed. Although it relaxes you at first, alcohol also dehydrates the body and disrupts natural sleep patterns. Good sleep hygiene also means keeping your bedroom quiet and dark and restful. If possible, avoid watching TV or using phones, laptops and tablets in bed. Taking a warm bath before bed, reading or even meditating are excellent ways to unwind and prepare for sleep. Eating disorders increase general anxiety levels, so deep breathing and relaxation exercises can also help, as can gentle yoga.

SOCIAL MEDIA

Social media has been a major driver in the rise of eating disorders, body dissatisfaction and general anxiety disorders. A 2016 UK government report found evidence of a 'slow-growing' epidemic of mental health issues in schools. They found that girls were twice as likely to have anxiety and depression as boys. They said they felt upset if their posts weren't 'liked' enough times, and felt they didn't look as good as their pretty, popular friends. One-third of girls in the government study of 30,000 teenagers showed symptoms of 'psychological distress'. Another 2016 study, from the charity Childline, found that social media pressures were leaving girls with 'crippling fears' about how they looked, and anxiety over body image that had grown by 17 per cent in the previous year. (See also **PEER PRESSURE**.) Marjorie Wallace, chief executive of the mental health charity Sane, cites the '24/7 exposure on social media' and its 'potentially destructive effect on issues such as self-esteem, body image or sex'.

For all its positive aspects – allowing millions of people around the word to communicate and collaborate – social media greatly contributes to the pressures of modern life, especially among the young. It fuels the damaging compare-and-despair syndrome, and exacerbates feelings of insecurity and worthlessness. This pressure appears to be particularly intense on those vulnerable to eating disorders, who are already highly anxious about their body shape or weight. They feel they should be working out harder for longer, should be eating cleaner or eating less; they should look like the vloggers, models or foodies they idolize. Sadly, social media is a gift to eating disorders, offering unrealistic images of the perfect food and fitness lifestyle, as well as persuasive product placement and celebrity endorsement. Internet sensations make a good living out of their YouTube channels, branding and aspirational glossy cookery shows, but the results are not achievable for most people.

It's important to distinguish between the online world and the real world. Eating disorders thrive on anxiety, comparison and insecurity, and there are thousands of carefully curated lifestyle blogs out there, ready to fuel these anxieties. But the realities of anorexia, bulimia and binge-eating are far from glamorous. No one Instagrams their downy face, swollen ankles, calloused fingers or decaying teeth.

Enjoy your life online, but remember to spend time in the real world too.

SOCIOTROPY

Excessive concern with acceptance by and approval from others.

SODIUM

Together with chloride, this mineral helps to regulate fluid balance, especially in the space outside the brain cells. Along with potassium, it is involved in nerve impulses, muscle contractions and the activity of the heart. The level of sodium is regulated by the kidneys, which eliminate any excess in the urine. Almost all foods contain sodium, either naturally occurring or as an ingredient added during processing or cooking. In cases of bulimia, excessive loss of sodium can occur through persistent vomiting or use of laxatives, leading to diarrhoea and dehydration. Signs of sodium deficiency include weakness, muscle cramps, confusion or fainting. In such cases, medical attention is always recommended. (See also **BULIMIA NERVOSA, DEHYDRATION, ELECTROLYTES** and **VOMITING**.)

STARVATION

There is growing evidence to suggest that repeated fluctuations in weight and constant yo-yo dieting increase the risk of heart disease, and that the risk of early death may be as high as in morbid obesity. Both of these findings were reported in the *New England Journal of Medicine*: researchers found that people whose weight fluctuated dramatically were more likely to experience heart disease, cardiac arrest, blocked arteries, angina, stroke or heart failure. After accounting for other factors, their risk of death was 124 per cent higher, heart attack 117 per cent higher and stroke 136 per cent higher.

The physical effects of starvation on the body include sensitivity to cold, chilblains, poor circulation, slow pulse and fainting spells, sleep disturbance, weak bladder, excess hair growth on the body, thinning bones leading to fractures, pain and deformity, amenorrhoea and infertility, stomach shrinking and pain, reduced gut function and increased constipation, sluggish bone marrow and anaemia, liver damage due to malnutrition leading to swollen ankles and legs, increased blood cholesterol levels, general exhaustion, muscle weakness and even collapse. Psychological effects of starvation include extreme low mood, pessimism and despair, becoming preoccupied with food and urges to overeat, lack of interest in forming relationships with others, poor concentration and mental functioning, impaired ability to think straight and problem solve, and even suicidal thoughts.

SUGAR

Many people who do *not* have an eating disorder *do* have a sweet tooth. However, for some people with bulimia and BED, cravings for sweet things are extremely powerful. This may become an addiction to sugar that feels almost uncontrollable: once you start eating sweet things, you feel you cannot stop.

Sugary foods are absorbed by the bloodstream more quickly than other substances. This increase in blood sugar leads to the hormone insulin being quickly released, which subsequently moves the sugar into the cells, causing blood sugar levels to drop. This leads to cravings to eat more sweet things, particularly if you are undernourished or your eating patterns are erratic. Danger foods include chocolate, cakes and biscuits, as well as sugary or artificially sweetened drinks.

It's normal to enjoy small amounts of sweet foods – most humans do – but it's not normal to crave large amounts of them. The solution is to regain control over your eating patterns by reintroducing regular mealtimes. Sitting down to balanced meals at regular intervals throughout the day helps to balance blood sugar levels and reduce cravings (see **EATING CONTROL** and **CRAVINGS**). Avoid buying specific 'danger' foods if they trigger binges, but don't exclude whole food groups as you will only crave them more. The aim is to rebalance your attitude and appetite!

SUICIDE

Sadly, this is one of the leading causes of death in individuals with eating disorders, possibly higher than in any other psychiatric disorder. Across studies, approximately 20–40 per cent of deaths in anorexia are thought to result from suicide. Those with bulimia and BED are also more likely than the general population to attempt suicide. The importance of getting professional help at the earliest possible stage cannot be overemphasized.

SUPERFOODS

This is an invented marketing term to describe certain foods, usually costly or unusual, that are perceived to be nutritionally superior. The list changes all the time, but recent so-called superfoods have included kale, rainbow chard, quinoa (see **QUINOA**), chia seeds, goji and acai berries, avocado, Medjool dates, bone broth, freekeh, bee pollen and maca powder. Outlandish claims are made for super-foods that they reverse ageing, overcome skin conditions, sleep or digestive complaints, boost brainpower and even cure cancer.

It's important to keep the 'superfood' hype in perspective. Eating more fresh fruit and vegetables is always healthier – but everyday carrots and apples are packed with vitamins and minerals too, and far cheaper. They are also less damaging to the environment than exotic wild superfoods that have been flown halfway around the world. Studies show that kale ranks as less nutritious than simple watercress or spinach. Vitamin-infused water or coconut water is unlikely to be any more hydrating than regular tap water. Treat 'superfood' claims with scepticism and focus on eating well. You don't need wheatgrass shots or Adriatic krill to make your skin glow. Instead, opt for cheaper, greener, locally sourced produce that tastes good. (See also **CLEAN EATING** and **ORTHOREXIA**.)

SUPPLEMENTS

Although there is no conclusive evidence on whether or not nutri-tional supplements are necessary, most experts agree that there is nothing wrong with taking a good-quality multivitamin. Indeed, some nutritionists claim that barely 1 in 10 people receives suffi-cient vitamins, minerals and essential fats from his or her diet for optimum health.

If this is correct, it seems logical that someone with a restricted diet or purgative behaviours should take supplements. However, food should always be the first line of defence. It is always healthier to obtain your nutrients from food, in its natural, 'bioavailable' form, than from pills. Severely restricting calorie intake, cutting out entire food groups or purging after eating leads to serious nutritional defi-ciencies that supplements cannot redress. As the Ayurvedic saying goes, 'let food be thy medicine'.

Some specific supplements deliver genuine benefits: iron is im-portant for those with anaemia, a condition that is fairly common among women of childbearing age, and in elderly or unwell individuals (see **IRON**). Vitamin D can be helpful in winter, in countries where there is limited daylight and in those prone to seasonal affective disorder (SAD). Some people find vitamin C or echinacea beneficial during the cold and flu season. And of course some supplements are considered essential, for example, folic acid before and during pregnancy, and vitamin K for newborn babies (see **VITAMIN K**). However, many of the miraculous claims made for supplements are unsubstantiated and misleading: the industry is highly lucrative and minimally regulated. Recommended daily amount (RDA) guidelines vary widely, as does the quality of brands on sale.

Some supplements may even be unsafe. For example, vitamin E and beta-carotene have been scientifically proven to be useless – even harmful – when taken in isolation, as the *Annals of Internal Medicine* reported in 2014. There are complex interactions between foods, vitamins and minerals that pills cannot necessarily replicate. Calcium, for example, depends on both magnesium and vitamin D to deliver its full benefit. Vitamin C and zinc may cause nausea, diarrhoea and stomach cramps. Too much selenium can lead to hair loss, gastrointestinal upset, fatigue and mild nerve damage.

If you are diagnosed with a genuine deficiency, you need to be honest with your doctor and yourself as to whether you are still actively restricting your food intake or over-exercising to create an energy deficit. Most supplementation (see **ZINC**) is pointless if you continue to restrict your food intake or purge after eating. Careful supplementation may help if you have been diagnosed with a deficiency or during periods of stress, depression or illness. But always consult a doctor or qualified nutritionist before taking supplements.

SUPPORT NETWORK

See **FAMILY, FRIENDS** and **COGNITIVE BEHAVIOURAL THERAPY**.

TEETH

Repeated vomiting in bulimia nervosa can lead to dental damage. Tooth colour may change from white to brown or grey, and teeth may decay, fall out or need to be removed. In bulimia, stomach acids and other gastric substances are brought into the mouth. Repeated exposure to these highly acidic substances will cause dental erosion, discoloration and loss of enamel (decalcification). Decay and peri-odontal disease may also occur, as as well as increased sensitivity to temperature. Consuming quantities of fizzy 'diet' drinks may exacerbate the problem.

Unlike some of the other physical side effects of eating disorders, dental complications are not reversible with a return to health. Once lost or decayed, teeth cannot be fully restored.

TESTOSTERONE

See **SEX**.

TRIGGERS

For an individual with an eating disorder, the term 'triggers' refers to situations that tend to set off typical self-harming behaviour – restricting, bingeing, over-exercising or self-injury.

Typical triggers include advertisements in public places showing very slim models, newspaper articles in which a recovered anorexic talks about how low her weight dropped to, a friend saying she's on a diet, excessive media focus on weight and body shape, magazines filled with low-calorie recipes or food labelling listing calorie and fat content. These are all normal aspects of modern life, but they can be experienced as triggers by someone who is highly anxious about food and weight gain and is in a vulnerable state.

There is no consensus over whether 'triggers' are a valid or useful concept within the context of eating disorders. Some individuals who have anorexia, bulimia or BED disagree with the notion of triggers and trigger warnings, while others claim that specific cues in their environment or people around them can 'trigger' their disordered behaviours or make it worse.

Sceptics argue that so-called triggers are in fact present for everyone: most young people are bombarded with images of super-slim models and celebrities online; everyone sees advertisements and television programmes. They argue that individuals need to take responsibility for their own recovery – whether that's avoiding celebrity magazines or ignoring food labelling – and that learning to ignore external triggers is far more effective than complaining about them. To sceptics, the fundamental concept of recovery is taking back control over how you react to what you see and hear, and not blaming your own disordered eating behaviours on the outside world.

Triggers are controversial because they relate to issues of victimhood, blame and responsibility. Of course, sceptics have a point: our society is increasingly obsessed with perfect female bodies, slimness, diets and weight loss, so the individual needs to learn to cope. It's certainly important and empowering to be able to say, 'I'm in charge of my own health, what I view, what I eat and what I do; I'm not going to let others knock me off course.'

However, understanding one's own personal triggers for problem behaviour can be beneficial. For some it might be boredom; for others it might be anxiety or feeling upset. Working alone or with a therapist, it's useful to track what leads up to a typical episode of bingeing or purging (see also **JOURNAL**). What happened to spark it off? What were the emotions you felt at the time? What food did you choose and how did you feel afterwards? Understanding the triggers that lead to an episode will help you to avoid or control them.

For example, triggers can be quite simple. An individual with anorexia steps on the scale in her therapist's office and finds she has gained half a pound in weight. She feels panicky and guilty and instantly decides to punish herself by not eating for the rest of the day and extending her afternoon session in the gym. Or an individual with BED goes to the supermarket after trying to diet all day and ends up buying large quantities of 'unsafe' foods such as cakes and biscuits.

In both cases, these triggers can be avoided. The therapist can weigh the patient but turn the scales around and the two of them can agree not to share the specific number during the anxious period of weight gain. The individual prone to BED can eat a nourishing lunch before going to the supermarket and make a shopping list he or she can follow. This will avoid the frantic hunger that leads to a loss of control (see **DEPRIVATION**). Meeting a friend after shopping is also a good strategy as being occupied helps distract from the desire to overeat. In both cases, understanding the personal trigger will help to prevent the same situation recurring. Being around other people gives the urge (to over-exercise or binge) a chance to fade. Some emotional triggers, such as family arguments, cannot always be avoided, but the damage can be reduced. Instead of exercising or bingeing, it might help to write your feelings down or ring a friend.

Avoiding triggers may seem like a cop-out, but it's not. This is about self-preservation, staying sane and doing what's right for you! If some friends talk endlessly about diets and how much they weigh, it makes sense to give them a wide berth while you're recovering from anorexia. If magazines or websites make you feel inadequate or 'fat', don't look at them. If staying with difficult relatives seems to trigger overeating and purging episodes, give yourself a break from them or limit seeing them to a day-visit. Triggers will fade, given time, as you start to recover.

u

UNIPOLAR DEPRESSION

This is similar in form to bipolar depression, but the manic phase is absent. The individual experiences the depressive periods without the swings to the elevated 'highs' or mania. (See also **BIPOLAR DISORDER**.)

URINATION

Emptying the bladder more than six to eight times daily is considered frequent urination. Frequent urination is commonly experienced by those with anorexia, partly because they may be drinking large quantities of water and partly because there is little food in the digestive system. This can be disruptive to daily life and even more so to sleep patterns at night. Once the underlying cause is addressed – that is, eating regular meals – the problem should resolve itself immediately. If you experience any other symptoms, such as pain or other urinary or bladder concerns, you should consult your GP.

VEGANISM

This diet (and lifestyle) excludes all meat and fish, as well as all animal by-products, including dairy, eggs and honey. Strict vegans also avoid material derived from animals, including leather, fur, wool and silk. They abstain from cosmetics, soaps and other everyday products containing or created from the body of any living or dead animal. Veganism is driven by health, environmental or ethical reasons – often a combination of all three. (See also **VEGETARIANISM**.)

VEGETARIANISM

The vegetarian diet excludes meat and fish and some other animal products, depending on the individual. Lacto-ovo-vegetarians eat both dairy products and eggs; this is the most common type of vegetarian diet. Lacto-vegetarians eat dairy products but avoid eggs. Ovo-vegetarians eat eggs but not dairy products. As well as health, environmental and ethical reasons for adopting a vegetarian diet, some religious and spiritual movements advocate this, notably Hinduism, Jainism and Buddhism.

Vegetarianism is increasingly popular among the general popu-lation. The *Meat Atlas* by Friends of the Earth and the Heinrich Böll Foundation cites figures as high as 375 million vegetarians worldwide, although estimates vary wildly. The growth of veg-etarian eating has been fuelled by environmental awareness, health concerns and greater variety of vegetarian cuisine in supermarkets and restaurants. Limiting meat consumption is also popular, with movements such as Meat-free Mondays, Veganuary (going vegan for January) and Flexitarianism, which encourages people to experiment with more vegetable and non-meat based diets.

Cutting back on red meat is considered healthy, especially in relation to the average Western diet. Humans do not need to eat meat or animal products as long as they consume a varied range of plant foods, including nuts and seeds, and many studies have shown that vegetarianism can provide complete and balanced nutrition. The demand for meat is increasing globally, however, as living standards rise, despite ever scarcer natural resources of water and land for cattle. Vegetarianism helps to alleviate these environmental pressures, as well as reducing animal cruelty.

However, it has been suggested that adopting a vegetarian or vegan diet may be a way of masking an eating disorder. It is considered a socially acceptable way of limiting the foods you can eat and provides a good excuse to avoid food. There are no exact figures on the prevalence of vegetarianism and veganism in those with eating disorders, but it is clear that many anorexics follow non-animal diets. The new eating disorder orthorexia often begins as vegetarianism, which then becomes veganism, which then morphs into an ever more restrictive diet (see **ORTHOREXIA** and **CLEAN EATING**).

There is no reason why someone with an eating disorder cannot remain vegetarian and regain healthy weight on a non-meat-, non-fish-based diet. To return to 'normal' eating as a vegan, however, does need more care. While many vegans (without eating disorders) are perfectly healthy and eat a good diet, many everyday products – in shops, cafés and restaurants – are still not vegan. Additionally, veganism excludes dairy products, which are rich sources of calcium (see **CALCIUM** and **OSTEOPOROSIS/OSTEOPENIA**.) These limitations can be problematic for someone in recovery from anorexia or orthorexia.

A vegetarian diet is often high in fibre, which protects against intestinal cancers, and low in saturated fats. Vegan diets, however, may be lacking in calcium and vitamin B_{12} (see **VITAMIN B**

VEGETARIANISM

GROUP). Symptoms of vitamin B_{12} deficiency or anaemia should be discussed with your doctor, who can advise on supplements, if necessary.

VITAMIN B GROUP

This group of vitamins is responsible for metabolic functioning, particularly converting and distributing energy efficiently around the body, and making red blood cells. B vitamins work together to break down the food we eat to release energy for everyday life. They keep the nervous system healthy and are essential for good skin and eyes. The Bs include vitamins B_1 (thiamine), B_2 (riboflavin), B_3 (niacin), B_7 (biotin), folic acid and B_{12}.

Vitamin B_{12} is unusual, as it is required in smaller amounts than any other vitamin: around 10 micrograms spread over a day is as much as the body needs. However, B_{12} is essential for the production of red blood cells in bone marrow, the body's utilization of folic acid and carbohydrates and the healthy functioning of the nervous system. Vitamin B_{12} is also important for maintaining normal energy levels, protecting against cognitive decline and heart disease and repairing DNA damage. B_{12} deficiency is more common among vegans and vegetarians because they do not consume B_{12}-rich animal products – but omnivores can also suffer.

Signs of vitamin B_{12} deficiency, also known as pernicious anaemia, include extreme fatigue, muscle weakness, pins and needles, pale skin, mental confusion or poor memory, dizziness, depression and paranoia. Diagnosis is usually by means of a simple blood test, and most of these symptoms are reversible on treatment. Long-term deficiency can cause damage to the nervous system, although this is extremely rare.

Natural food sources of B_{12} include liver, kidney, chicken, beef, pork, fish, eggs, dairy products such as milk and yogurt, and yeast extracts such as Marmite. Vegans and vegetarians should prioritize foods fortified with B_{12}, including some plant milks, some soya products and some breakfast cereals, and take B_{12} supplements if necessary.

VITAMIN DEFICIENCIES

See **SUPPLEMENTS**.

VITAMIN K

This vitamin is actually several different vitamins, K_1 and K_2 being the most important. It plays an essential role in blood clotting to prevent excessive bleeding and promote wound healing. It is also needed as a calcium binder to produce strong bones, helping to prevent bone weakness and fractures.

Vitamin K is generally obtained through eating a varied diet. Natural food sources include green leafy vegetables such as spinach, kale, broccoli and asparagus, beans and soya beans, fruits including avocado, grapes and strawberries, eggs and meat. Vitamin K is fat-soluble, which means that its absorption by the body is greatly increased when consumed with some fat: a little butter or oil with green leafy vegetables, for example. Individuals with a restrictive eating disorder generally avoid all forms of fat and this can interfere with the absorption of this important vitamin.

Unlike other vitamins, vitamin K is rarely taken as a dietary supplement and deficiency is rare in adults. (Newborn babies are given a vitamin K injection soon after birth.) However, vitamin K deficiency is a risk for those with impaired gut absorption, such as in coeliac disease, and in cystic fibrosis, chronic kidney disease and liver damage, for example, caused by cirrhosis or alcohol abuse. Vitamin K deficiency is also a risk for those with eating disorders, particularly individuals who have bulimia, who are malnourished or have osteoporosis.

Symptoms of vitamin K deficiency are usually related to problematic blood clotting: bleeding within the digestive tract, bleeding gums, heavy menstrual bleeding or haemorrhaging. Bruising very easily can also be a sign of deficiency.

Any concerns over excessive bleeding or bruising should be discussed with a medical professional before starting to take any vitamin K supplements.

VOMITING

Regular self-induced vomiting is not only unpleasant for the individual, it's also extremely dangerous (see **DEHYDRATION**, **ELECTROLYTES** and **CARDIAC COMPLICATIONS**). Vomiting may rid the body of 30–50 per cent of calories eaten, depending on how soon after eating it happens. However, the more you vomit, the more you will crave food, which creates a vicious cycle of more bingeing and more purging. Vomiting is never a safe or sustained method of weight loss.

The body is naturally designed to consume and digest food, taking the essential nutrients it requires and then eliminating unwanted waste matter via the bladder and bowel. Except when we are unwell (or if we have been poisoned), we are not designed to get rid of food by vomiting. Vomiting puts the body under significant stress. Repeated and violent vomiting damages the stomach and oesophagus by causing ruptures or tears in the lining, causing the individual to vomit blood. Bleeding is a serious symptom and must always be investigated: in severe bulimia, internal bleeding can cause death.

Vomiting causes red, bloodshot eyes and broken blood vessels around the eyes and in the face. Frequent vomiting affects the salivary glands, resulting in a puffy 'chipmunk'-like appearance of the cheeks. Vomiting also causes callouses on the fingers, from putting them down the throat. Mouth ulcers and sore throats are another common side effect of repeated vomiting.

Acid reflux is a painful problem, caused by the continual loosening of the valve that normally prevents food from leaving the stomach. The acid therefore moves up the oesophagus, resulting in a burning sensation. This acid reflux, and repeated exposure to stomach acid, damages the oesophagus and has even been linked to oesophageal cancer.

WEIGHT GAIN

Although recovery from disordered eating involves a significant mental component, in conditions such as anorexia there is no substitute for weight gain. CBT and other forms of therapy can provide psychological support during the recovery process, but there is no avoiding the fundamental issue: to beat anorexia, you have to eat. To put it another way, weight gain is not a magic cure if you don't address the underlying emotional issues, but, equally, if you don't restore your body to a healthy weight, recovery is impossible.

Recovery is inexplicably difficult, however: it involves an acceptance that the scales will increase, tiny clothes may become tighter – and it involves a commitment to maintaining that higher body weight. It involves challenging beliefs about one's body and oneself, giving up private, disordered habits around food and an acceptance that maybe 'normal' is OK. All the psychological and theoretical insights in the world cannot replace the body's simple need for adequate nutrition and regular rest. Many 'recovering' anorexics secretly maintain damaging behaviours. This is futile and self-sabotaging.

Weight gain takes different forms. For many, it will be a gradual process of widening the food horizons, cutting back on excessive exercise and allowing the body to find its natural healthy weight (see **SET POINT THEORY**). In cases of severe anorexia nervosa, individuals may be admitted to an inpatient clinic or hospital. With specialist care from doctors, therapists and dietitians, they can be supported to regain a healthy body weight (see **REFEEDING**).

Whatever the setting, the focus is on steady, manageable weight gain, usually set by clinicians at around 2 to 3 pounds per week, although this will depend on individual circumstances. Many individuals with anorexia want to gain weight more slowly than this (so as to stay in control), but this only prolongs the process.

Weight gain is frightening for an individual with anorexia. This may not make sense to outsiders, who only see a desperately underweight patient who needs to eat, but it can be an agonizing process. Not only are individuals being monitored at every meal, forced to consume high-calorie foods and to eat with others, but they are also prevented from over-exercising and are encouraged to rest, especially after meals. Everything they have relied upon – controlling every calorie that passes their lips and instantly burning it off – is reversed. They are congratulated on weight gain when it feels to them like failure.

Unfortunately, many weight-gain programmes have limited success in the long term. The perennial problem here – and the reason anorexia remains such a stubborn, chronic condition – is that weight gain is often temporary. A significant proportion of anorexic individuals who are discharged following weight gain will simply lose the weight again on returning home. For this reason, successful treatment of anorexia is a complicated balancing act between physical and psychological recovery, and ongoing emotional support.

WELLNESS

This has come to mean more than just the opposite of illness! 'Wellness' is a term popular with the clean eating movement to convey a blissful state of dietary virtue and glowing health. Wellness is a lifestyle, an image and a lucrative marketing angle for everything from fitness wear and gyms to superfoods and spiralizers. Wellness is aspirational and seductively photogenic: you will see #wellness hashtags all over Instagram – along with perfect yoga poses, expensive athleisure wear and glowing smiles. (See also **CLEAN EATING** and **ORTHOREXIA**.)

WILLPOWER

In our culture, willpower is considered to be a positive trait. Those who run ultra-marathons have admirable willpower, as do those who climb mountains or sail single-handed around the world. However, in those with anorexia, willpower can be life-threatening.

It does take willpower not to eat – after all, hunger is the most natural and basic of human instincts. Food is our source of life. But when you take this willpower to extremes, as in self-starvation, it is dangerous. However, willpower can be turned around and used to rebuild, not destroy, your life. Instead of using your willpower to withstand hunger, use it to regain your health.

XEROPHAGY

This is the eating of dry food only, including food cooked without oil. Xerophagy was a form of fasting practised in the early Christian church.

YOGA

Restrictive eating and fear of weight gain often go hand in hand with compulsive exercise. Indeed, many anorexic individuals intensify their physical activity to cope with the stress of enforced weight gain. When they find themselves in treatment, they are often prevented from doing any exercise at all, which is tough. They have relied on exercise not only as a way of burning off calories, but also to alleviate depression and anxiety. We are surrounded by headlines and health warnings extolling the virtues of physical activity – and everyone enjoys the endorphin boost of exercise, whatever their weight.

However, you do not need to stop exercising completely. Gentler forms such as yoga and pilates can provide the psychological benefits of physical exercise without causing further weight loss. Controlled, gentle exercise will strengthen the musculoskeletal system and prevent further bone deterioration (see **OSTEOPOROSIS/OSTEO-PENIA**). It can also help with improved body image and the development of new interests.

The focus of exercise in recovery should be on enjoyment and social interaction, rather than on burning off calories. High-intensity, solitary exercise such as running is not on the menu! Instead, group exercise is ideal – in particular yoga. There are many different forms of yoga and it is essential to speak to a qualified instructor about your illness and where you are in your recovery. You should avoid vigorous or 'dynamic' forms, such as Vinyasa or Ashtanga. You must also avoid any hot 'Bikram'-style classes as these could be extremely dangerous because of, for example, cardiac stress, dehydration and so on.

Hatha yoga focuses on slow and gentle movements and is ideal for combatting stress and anxiety, and for winding down at the end of the day. It covers all the basic asanas (postures), so it's a good place to start if you're a beginner. Restorative yoga includes simple poses supported by pillows and focuses on relaxation, so it's ideal for unwinding and learning how to quieten your mind.

As well as the therapeutic physical benefits of yoga, many people find it provides a mental, even 'spiritual', workout. There is a great deal of stress and pain involved in mental illness and recovery and yoga can really help. At its best, yoga is self-accepting, nurturing and healing – everything that eating disorders are not. Yoga emphasizes the mind–body connection, which is often profoundly disturbed in those with eating disorders. Yoga develops mental and emotional strength as well as physical flexibility. It isn't just about bending and stretching and holding a pose, it's about staying in an unaccustomed position, literally learning to be in a difficult place. And many of the techniques you practise on the yoga mat can be applied to everyday situations: deep breathing to help with panic attacks or insomnia, for example, or holding on when you want to give up.

Any exercise regime will depend on the severity of your illness and should only be started once you begin to gain weight and in consultation with your care team. No one should be practising yoga if they are still undereating, nor should they be taking multiple classes a day.

Z

ZERO, SIZE

The term 'size zero' derives from female clothing sizes and is widely used to describe the bodies of women, usually models or celebrities, who are extremely thin. US size 0 and 00 are part of the general trend to reduce clothing sizes – also known as vanity sizing. US size 0 is roughly equivalent to a UK size 4, US size 2 is about a UK size 6, US size 4 the equivalent of a UK size 8 and so on.

The size zero trend has been blamed for the proliferation of eating disorders among adolescent girls and young women and has even been linked to high-profile deaths among underweight fashion models. In response to the size zero backlash, several fashion weeks, including in Madrid and Milan, have banned models with a BMI below 18.

ZINC

Zinc is a micronutrient (trace element) involved in normal growth, development of the reproductive organs, healing of wounds and manufacture of proteins and nucleic acids in the body. It is involved in the functioning of the hormone insulin and in controlling the activity of over 100 enzymes.

Small amounts of zinc can be found in lean meat, wholemeal bread, wholegrain cereals, dried beans and seafood.

Loss of appetite is a typical symptom of zinc deficiency. This interesting fact appears to have led to confusion over whether or not zinc deficiency might cause eating disorders. It has been suggested, although not proven, that zinc deficiency may play a part in the onset of anorexia and bulimia nervosa. Bear in mind, however, that true zinc deficiency is rare. Most instances occur in cases of malnutrition: in other words, the anorexia or bulimia is the problem, not the zinc itself.

Scientific trials going back several decades have shown up to double the amount of weight restoration among anorexic patients given zinc supplementation compared with those given a placebo (an inactive dummy tablet). However, this zinc link should be taken with several caveats. First, it is not known whether the weight gain was maintained or whether the patient relapsed into restrictive behaviours after the study. Second, the anorexic patients were under medical supervision and following 'recovery' eating plans. As previously explained (see **SUPPLEMENTS**), taking zinc in the context of a severely restricted regime will not work. Any supplement should be added to, not used instead of, a healthy diet.

Again, taking high levels of a specific micronutrient is not always useful or safe. For example, if you do not have a zinc deficiency and begin taking it as a supplement, you risk creating a copper deficiency that may lead to anaemia. Some individuals with anorexia may have a zinc deficiency, but this is more likely to be due to malnutrition and a general lack of nutrients obtained from food. As with all supplements, seek medical advice first.

ZINC